YORK NOTES

General Editors: Professor A.N. Jeffares (*University of Stirling*) & Professor Suheil Bushrui (*American University of Beirut*)

William Shakespeare

HENRY V

Notes by Charles Barber

MA (CAMBRIDGE) PH D (GOTHENBURG)
Formerly Reader in English Language and Literature, University of Leeds

LONGMAN
YORK PRESS

The illustration of the Globe Playhouse on page 13 is from *The Globe Restored in Theatre: A Way of Seeing* by C. Walter Hodges, published by Oxford University Press © Oxford University Press.

YORK PRESS
Immeuble Esseily, Place Riad Solh, Beirut

LONGMAN GROUP LIMITED
Longman House, Burnt Mill, Harlow,
Essex CM20 2JE, England
Associated companies, branches and representatives
throughout the world

© Librairie du Liban 1980

First published 1980
Tenth impression 1994

ISBN 0-582-78135-3

Produced by Longman Singapore Publishers Pte Ltd
Printed in Singapore

Contents

Part 1: Introduction *page* 5

The historical background 5
The social hierarchy 5
The Elizabethan world-view 7
Man's salvation 8
The middle way of Queen Elizabeth I 8
The equilibrium of the 1590s 9
The Elizabethan drama 10
The Elizabethan public theatre 12
The literary background 14
William Shakespeare 15
Shakespeare's history plays 16
A note on the text 17

Part 2: Summaries 19

A general summary 19
Detailed summaries 19

Part 3: Commentary 48

Date and sources 48
Medieval and Tudor kings 48
Patriotic feeling 50
A play of outer action 52
The ideal Christian king 53
Henry the man 55
Is the play ironic? 56
A critical light on the war 57
The absence of politics 58
The absence of Falstaff 60
The other characters 61
The language of the play 65

Part 4: Hints for study 67
  General advice 67
  Topics for study 68
  Essay questions 69
  Writing an essay 69
  Specimen essay plan 70
  Specimen essay 71

Part 5: Suggestions for further reading 74

The author of these notes 77

Part 1

Introduction

The historical background

William Shakespeare lived from 1564 to 1616. During his lifetime there was a period of relative stability and peace in English society. This period of calm occurred between two periods of tumult and change, the Reformation and the Civil Wars. The Reformation was the breaking away of the English church from the authority of the Pope in Rome, followed by changes in religious doctrine and church services. It was started by King Henry VIII about twenty-five years before Shakespeare was born. There followed a period of conflict between Protestants (reformers) and Catholics (traditionalists), breaking out at times into armed rebellion, both under the Protestant King Edward VI (1547–53) and under the Catholic Queen Mary (1553–58). Twenty-five years after Shakespeare's death, England was just entering the Civil Wars (1640–49), the armed struggle between King and Parliament which can well be called the English Revolution.

The Reformation and the Civil Wars were major stages in the change from feudal England to capitalist England. In Shakespeare's lifetime, English society still had feudal forms and a feudal social structure, but within this society there were powerful forces for change. There were Puritans, who wished to carry the Reformation further and to abolish bishops; there were scientists, who were undermining traditional views of the universe; and above all there were capitalist landlords and merchants who, especially in south-eastern England, were trying to break down or evade the customary controls on economic activity.

The age of Shakespeare, then, was one both of stability and of tension; and both these factors exercised a strong effect on his art. The period of relative calm and prosperity in the second half of the reign of Elizabeth I (1558–1603) provided material conditions in which a professional English theatre could flourish; the social tensions provided, if only indirectly, the subject-matter for the greatest plays of this theatre.

The social hierarchy

In English society in Shakespeare's time there was a well-defined hierarchy, that is, a series of graded ranks. In theory, every individual belonged to one of these grades. Four main grades were usually recognised: (*i*) gentlemen, (*ii*) citizens, (*iii*) yeomen, and (*iv*) artificers and labourers. The second group, citizens, did not include everybody who worked in a town, but only those who were masters of their trade; it thus excluded journeymen (craftsmen hired by the masters, and paid a daily wage) and also apprentices. The third group, the yeomen, were substantial farmers; they had to hold land worth at least forty shillings a year; unlike gentlemen-landlords, they engaged in manual labour on their farms. The fourth group included all kinds of wage-labourers, and peasants who were not substantial enough to qualify as yeomen.

The first group, that of the gentlemen, consisted of a considerable number of graded ranks. At the top was the prince (or sovereign); then came the peers or the nobility (dukes, marquises, earls, viscounts, barons); and finally the lesser gentry (knights, esquires, gentlemen). It will be noticed that the word *gentleman*, which was of enormous importance in Shakespeare's England, had more than one meaning. First, it can mean anybody in the top group of society, including knights, noblemen, and even the monàrch: in *Henry V*, Pistol claims to be 'as good a gentleman as the Emperor' (IV.1.42). But secondly, *gentleman* was used as the name of one sub-group in this class, namely the lowest, the simple gentleman; this use of the word is seen in *Henry V* when the king is given a list of the French dead after Agincourt, consisting of 'princes ... nobles ... knights, esquires, and gallant gentlemen' (IV.8.80–84).

The gentlemen (in the wide sense) probably represented only about five per cent of the population, but they had almost all the power, and many privileges. In essence they were a land-owning class, but certain other groups were also recognised as gentlemen, for example army officers of the rank of captain and above, and people with university degrees (though there was always some dispute about the exact boundaries).

When we read Shakespeare, we have to remember that words like *gentle* and *noble* often refer to social class, as do words like *mechanic, base, common,* and *vulgar* (all of which refer to people of the lowest class). Before Agincourt, Pistol asks the disguised king

> art thou officer,
> *Or art thou base, common, and popular?*
> (IV.1.37–38)

Immediately before the battle, in his speech of encouragement, Henry says

> *he today that sheds his blood with me*
> *Shall be my brother; be he ne'er so vile,*
> *This day shall gentle his condition.*
> (IV.3.61–63)

He means that anybody fighting at Agincourt, however low (*vile*) his social rank (*condition*), will thereby gain the social status of a gentleman.

In practice, the social system was more complicated than the four-class picture suggests. Moreover, the class-barriers were not rigid, and there was movement both up and down. Nevertheless, the status of gentleman was a key one, and the reader of Shakespeare has to learn to respond to the implications of words like *gentle*.

The Elizabethan world-view

The dominant beliefs of the age reflect the hierarchial forms of society, and the idea of order or hierarchy is central. The whole universe formed one vast hierarchy, from God down to the minerals; there were no gaps in the chain, and everything had a place in it. Below God were the angels, arranged in nine ranks; then human beings; then three grades of animal life; then vegetable life; and finally inanimate objects. Man was a key point in the whole chain, the link between matter and spirit, and he constituted a kind of miniature universe, a microcosm. There were detailed resemblances between his body and the universe. For example, the universe was believed to be made of four elements (earth, air, fire, water), composed of pairs of four fundamental qualities (hot, cold, moist, dry). Similarly, a man's temperament was thought to be determined by the balance within him of four fluids, called humours (melancholy, blood, choler, phlegm), composed of the same four qualities. The hierarchies that composed the universe were similar to one another in various ways: as God was head of the universe, so the king was head of society, the lion the king of beasts, the eagle the king of birds, the sun the chief of the heavenly bodies, the head the chief part of the human body, and so on.

According to this world-view, it is natural for people to accept their place in the social hierarchy: it is natural (and therefore right) for subjects to obey their king, for women to obey their husbands, for children to obey their parents. The use of the natural orderliness of the universe to justify obedience to the established social order is illustrated by the famous account in *Henry V* of the honey-bees (I.2.184–204). The Archbishop of Canterbury describes the orderliness found in a hive, where each bee has a naturally determined social function (magistrate, merchant, soldier, mason, citizen, porter ...), all under a single king; this is a model for a human society, where the class-system is similarly ordained by God, and obedience is a prime virtue.

Man's salvation

There were bitter religious disputes in sixteenth-century England, but it was still taken for granted that everybody in the country was a Christian, and accepted a certain religious view of the universe. According to this view, the universe had a purpose: it had been created for the benefit of mankind, and it was the stage for the drama of man's salvation. When God created Adam and Eve and placed them in the Garden of Eden, they were perfect and sinless. Then came the Fall of Man: at the instigation of the serpent, Adam and Eve disobeyed God and became sinful. Without sin, mankind would have been immortal, but the result of sin is death. Moreover, sinfulness is inherited, so that all mankind are inherently sinful, and subject to death. The punishment for sin is eternal damnation in Hell, but God has redeemed mankind from this punishment: he himself came to earth and suffered death by crucifixion, thus taking upon himself the punishment due to mankind. All those who believe in him are forgiven their sins, and will escape Hell, going instead to eternal bliss in Heaven. At the end of the world will come the Last Judgement: God, surrounded by his angels, will descend to the earth; the dead will arise from their graves, and God will sit in judgement on every member of mankind.

The middle way of Queen Elizabeth I

The social and political conflicts of the age tended to be fought out in the arena of religion. On the one hand there were the Puritans, who wished to remove from the church what they considered to be relics of paganism. On the other hand there were the Catholics, who wanted to restore older forms of worship and once again recognise the Pope as the head of the English church. Catholicism was illegal in England in Elizabeth's reign, since Catholics did not recognise Elizabeth as the legitimate queen; but it was still a strong force, especially in the more feudal north, while puritanism was strongest in the south-east and in the great seaports.

Elizabeth maintained her position by constant compromise, and by holding the balance of power between the contending parties. Her policy of compromise is well illustrated by her church settlement. It was still universally accepted that there could be only one church in England, compulsory for all; the disputes were about the nature of this church. Elizabeth's settlement tried to make the Church of England acceptable to as many people as possible. The monarch was head of the church, and it was governed by bishops, thus maintaining the forms of a hierarchical society; but many disputed points of doctrine were deliberately left ambiguous. From most of the population, Elizabeth demanded only an outward conformity, saying that she had no 'windows on men's souls'. The Church of England, not unnaturally, was attacked from both sides, Catholic and Puritan, but aimed at conciliating the moderates in both camps.

In the 1580s, after some years of relative stability in England, there was a growing sense of national unity and national pride. These feelings were greatly encouraged by the events of 1588. In that year, Spain, the most powerful of the Catholic countries, attempted to invade England with an army carried in an enormous fleet, the so-called Great Armada. The Armada was crushingly defeated by the English navy: of 129 ships that left Spain, only 54 battered wrecks returned. But, what was perhaps more important, the expected Catholic revolt did not take place. Nobody knew how many secret Catholics there were in England, nor what percentage of them belonged to the militant wing that advocated armed rebellion. But the ruling classes certainly feared such a revolt, and it was this fear that led many advanced Protestants and many capitalist landlords to support the Crown. When the Spanish fleet sailed up the English Channel, many people expected a major rising; but in the event the Catholic rebellion just did not materialise; and the euphoria of the years following 1588, the exhilaration and the sense of national unity, were surely due as much to this fact as to the defeat of the Armada.

The equilibrium of the 1590s

But the moment of national unity contained the seeds of its own decay. If there was no longer any danger of a Catholic counter-revolution, there was no longer any need for Puritans or capitalist gentry to support the Crown: and the stage was set for the coming conflict between Crown and Parliament. But for ten or fifteen years after the Armada there was an uneasy truce, partly because of the long war against Spain, partly because many men were content to wait for the old queen to die, hoping for better things from her successor. So there was a period of equilibrium, like the interval between an ebbing and a flowing tide. Then in the early seventeenth century, social forces became more and more polarised, and the struggle for power began between King and Parliament, to culminate in the Civil Wars.

It will be seen that Shakespeare's career as a dramatist, which ran from about 1590 to 1612, occurred at a critical point in English history. The first decade of his writing occurred in the upsurge of national confidence and exhilaration which followed the defeat of the Armada, when class-conflicts were temporarily damped down and there was a strong sense of national unity. In the theatre, these feelings are reflected in the popularity of history-plays, which usually handle the events of

England's past in a patriotic manner; they are a common theatrical type until about 1605, after which time they almost entirely disappear. Shakespeare's *Henry V* (1599) belongs to this period, and can be seen as a celebration of national unity and patriotic feeling. In the 1590s, besides history-plays, Shakespeare mainly writes romantic comedies, tragedies being the exception. But in about 1600, when England begins to move into a period of social crisis and conflict, Shakespeare's work shows a marked change: between 1600 and 1610 his works are predominantly tragedies, and even plays which are nominally comedies are in fact really problem-plays. In the plays of this period, Shakespeare explores the growing social crisis of the time, not directly, but through ideas, attitudes, conflicting world-views.

The Elizabethan drama

Shakespeare was not an isolated phenomenon: he was the greatest figure in a theatrical industry which employed dozens of writers and produced hundreds of plays. Even if Shakespeare had never lived, the period from 1585 to 1625 would still have been a great age of English drama. The basis for this achievement was the existence of a number of permanent theatres and theatrical companies in London, and of a large audience for them. The theatres performed every afternoon except Sunday, and put on a different play every day: a new play was not given a continuous run, but was revived for single performances, the intervals between revivals getting greater as its popularity declined. The standards of performance were high: the London theatre was a full-time professional theatre, and its actors were famous all over northern Europe.

The first two specially-built public theatres in London, the Theatre and the Curtain, were built in 1576. At that time Shakespeare was twelve years old, and by the time he reached manhood the London theatre was an established institution, with its companies, its audiences, its conventions—an institution sufficiently stable and respectable to attract to its service an ambitious young man from the provinces with literary inclinations.

The theatres built in 1576 did not spring up suddenly out of nothing: there was already a centuries-old tradition of popular drama in England—religious plays, folk-festival plays, moral plays with allegorical characters. Alongside these arose in the sixteenth century a more learned drama: at schools and universities, students performed plays by Latin authors (Terence, Plautus, Seneca), and then English plays in imitation of them. There were also various kinds of entertainment at court, and by the 1580s elegant and stylish prose comedies were being performed at the court of Elizabeth I. So in the second half of the sixteenth century there was a profusion of dramatic traditions in England—religious and secular, popular and polite, academic and courtly.

One consequence of the period of national unity and social equilibrium of the 1580s and 1590s was that the theatre became genuinely national, addressing itself to all classes of society. University men went into the popular theatre as writers, and brought about a fusion of the popular and academic and courtly traditions. An example of this is Christopher Marlowe (1564–93), who went to the University of Cambridge, taking his BA degree in 1584 and his MA in 1587; he then wrote a series of famous and successful tragedies for the London theatre, of which the best known is *Dr Faustus* (*c*. 1592). The fusion of traditions was possible because there was also a fusion of audiences: the theatre that Shakespeare wrote for represented all the classes of London, from noblemen down to labourers, and their womenfolk. And when Shakespeare's company performed for the Queen at court, they acted for her the same plays as those performed for the audience of their public theatre.

With the fusion of traditions, the great period of the English drama begins. The broad audience was one of the theatre's sources of strength. For maximum success, plays needed the sophistication and elegance demanded by the gentry in the audience, but also the directness of appeal and the entertainment-value demanded by the uneducated. The fact that the best dramatists of the age could fulfil these requirements suggests that the different social groups in the audience had a remarkable similarity in their outlook and interests.

But, like the equilibrium in society, the wide audience of Shakespeare's theatre was the product of just one moment in history, and then passed away. In the opening years of the seventeenth century, the single broad audience of the 1590s began to split into two different audiences: a courtly audience at the more expensive indoor theatres, and a more popular audience at the old public theatres. Shakespeare's theatre, the Globe, with its great prestige, probably managed to retain a broad audience until the end of his theatrical career. But within a few years of his death, the old public theatres had sunk to crude and noisy places where simple entertainment was given for the artisan classes, while purpose-built indoor theatres catered for people of the highest rank and fashion. Under the influence of the rising tide of puritanism, the middle section had dropped out of the audience, leaving a plebeian audience on the one hand, and a courtly audience on the other. Such different theatres demanded very different kinds of play, and the synthesis of popular, learned, and courtly traditions gradually disintegrated.

The Elizabethan public theatre

The public theatres for which most of Shakespeare's plays were written were small, wooden, open-air theatres, in which the plays were performed by daylight. The width of a theatre was always as great as its length: it could be round, or square, but not oblong. The Fortune Theatre was eighty feet square outside, and fifty-five feet square inside, and this was probably a typical size. A theatre consisted of three tiers of covered galleries surrounding an open central arena. From one side, the main stage projected half-way into the arena, partly protected from the weather by a roof supported at the front by two pillars. The actors came on to the stage through large doors on each side of the back wall. They were very close to the audience, which was on three sides of the stage: some spectators stood in the arena, while others had seats in the galleries. For obvious technical reasons, there was no front curtain to the large projecting stage, so scenes began and ended simply by the entry and exit of the characters. In the back wall behind the main stage was a small inner stage concealed by curtains: here a character could hide and spy on others, or the curtains could be opened to reveal people or things hitherto concealed from the audience. Above this inner stage, at the level of the middle tier of audience galleries, was an upper stage, which could be used to represent a balcony or an upstairs window or the walls of a town. In *Henry V* (III.3) the Governor of Harfleur parleys with King Henry: the scene was probably played with the Governor on the upper stage, as if on the wall, and with Henry on the main stage below him.

Elizabethan theatres made little use of scenery. Portable furniture, like chairs and tables, could be carried on to the stage, and sometimes a bed was pushed on; but no attempt was made to construct realistic sets. Nor, since the performances were in daylight, was use made of lighting-effects. On the other hand, the theatre did make considerable use of music and of sound-effects (like the alarums and cannon and trumpet-calls in *Henry V*), and of splendid costumes (which were usually Elizabethan ones, with no attempt at historical accuracy). Predominantly, however, the theatre depended on the spoken word: it was a word-centred and actor-centred drama.

Because of the absence of scenery and of a front curtain, the action of the play could flow continuously without any break between the scenes, like a film. As the actors walked off the stage at the end of one scene, another group of actors came in by a different door for the next one. In Act IV of *Henry V*, in which the battle takes place, there are eight different scenes; but these must be played without any break. Nor is it necessary for a scene to take place in a clearly defined location. If the audience needs to know the location, it will be indicated by the speakers; but often there is no indication. Modern editions of the plays often give a location at the beginning of each scene ('Act I Scene 1. London. An Antechamber in the King's Palace'); but these locations have been added by modern editors, and are not found in the original editions.

The theatre had developed a number of conventions of its own, for all drama rests on unstated assumptions which have to be accepted by the audience. Such conventions are the aside and the soliloquy. In the aside, we have to accept that a character can make a speech which is

THE GLOBE PLAYHOUSE

The theatre, originally built by James Burbage in 1576, was made of wood (Burbage had been trained as a carpenter). It was situated to the north of the River Thames on Shoreditch in Finsbury Fields. There was trouble with the lease of the land, and so the theatre was dismantled in 1598, and reconstructed 'in an other forme' on the south side of the Thames as the Globe. Its sign is thought to have been a figure of the Greek hero Hercules carrying the globe. It was built in six months, its galleries being roofed with thatch. This caught fire in 1613 when some smouldering wadding, from a cannon used in a performance of Shakespeare's *Henry VIII*, lodged in it. The theatre was burnt down, and when it was rebuilt again on the old foundations, the galleries were roofed with tiles.

heard by the audience but not by the other characters on the stage; it is a way of revealing what a character is thinking. In the soliloquy, the character is alone on the stage, and utters his thoughts aloud for the audience to hear, as Henry V does in his speech on ceremony (IV.1.223–77); it is moreover one of the conventions that, in a soliloquy, the character speaks the truth and reveals himself as he really is. Another convention of the Elizabethan stage is that a character can sometimes talk in verse, and sometimes in prose.

The literary background

However broad the audience of the public theatre, the men who wrote the plays for it in Shakespeare's time were usually men of education. Shakespeare himself did not have a university education, but it is clear from his work that he had been to a grammar school, and that, while not a scholar, he was steeped in the learning of his time.

By the late sixteenth century, English education was dominated by the ideas of the so-called humanists, ideas which had arisen in Italy in the late Middle Ages and gradually spread to northern Europe. Basically, Renaissance humanism was the belief in a certain type of education, namely one based on the pagan classics—the poetry, drama, oratory, history, and philosophy of ancient Greece and Rome. In practice, it was Roman civilisation which was dominant. In Elizabethan grammar schools, the pupils were taught not only to read and write Latin, but also to speak it. They read Latin authors, with especial emphasis on poetry, and were taught to analyse literary texts by the methods of classical rhetoric. Rhetoric was originally the art of oratory, speech-making, but even in antiquity its methods and procedures had been applied to literature too, and in the Renaissance the handbooks of rhetoric were commonly regarded as handbooks for poets. The pupils were also taught some elementary logic, based on that of Aristotle, the ancient Greek philosopher who was one of the major influences on European thought in the Middle Ages and the Renaissance; and logic, like rhetoric, was applied to the techniques of reading and writing literature.

When university men began to write for the public theatres in the 1580s, this classical influence entered the popular drama. It is seen, for example, in the structure of plays, notably in the use of the five-act pattern inherited from Roman comedy; in the free use of classical allusions, especially allusions to mythology (the legendary stories of gods and ancient heroes); in the taking over of stock characters from Latin dramatists; and in the influence of classical rhetoric on style. One of the stock characters borrowed from Roman comedy was the *miles gloriosus*, the boastful soldier; Elizabethan dramatists produced many variants of this character, Pistol in *Henry V* being one. The aspect of rhetoric that was most influential was the figure of speech, and figures of all kinds were cultivated with enthusiasm by late-Elizabethan poets. They were especially fond of verbal patterns, achieved by various kinds of repetition. Shakespeare's earliest plays are full of patterns of this kind, but by the time of *Henry V* the fashion for this rather obvious stylistic device was receding. Nevertheless, Shakespeare still uses it occasionally (see for example I.2.209–11, II.2.127-31). A different kind of figure is seen in Fluellen's elaborate comparison of Henry V with Alexander the Great (IV.7.11-51), which is carried out according to the best rules of rhetoric, but becomes comic because of the incongruity of the comparisons.

William Shakespeare

Shakespeare was born in 1564 in Stratford-on-Avon, a West Midland market-town of about two thousand inhabitants. His father, John Shakespeare, came from a family of yeomen outside Stratford, but had moved into the town and become a glover, eventually owning his own shop. He prospered, bought property, and was elected to various civic offices; and in 1568-69 he was Bailiff, the chief civic dignitary of Stratford. We know nothing of William's boyhood, but there can be little doubt that, as the son of a prosperous citizen, he went to Stratford Grammar School, which was a good school and free for the sons of Stratford citizens. In 1582 he married Anne Hathaway, a yeoman's daughter, by whom he had three children.

Apart from his christening, his marriage, and the birth of his children, we have no firm knowledge of Shakespeare's life until 1592, when an attack on him by Robert Greene shows that he was already a dramatist of some reputation in London. His earliest plays date from about 1589, and he probably went to London and became an actor there not long before that date. For Shakespeare was not like the university men who wrote for the theatre without belonging to it: he was an actor and professional man of the theatre, and it was on the success of a theatrical company that his fortunes were founded. His plays were doubtless one of the great assets of his company, but it was his position as a 'sharer' in the outstanding theatrical company of the day that made him a man of substance.

London theatrical companies were organised on a co-operative basis: a number of actors (the sharers) invested jointly in the necessary equipment (books, properties), hired a theatre, and shared the proceeds after each performance. The sharers did most of the acting themselves, but they could also hire journeymen actors, and for the women's parts they had boys, who had the status of apprentices; there were no actresses in Shakespeare's time. For legal reasons each company needed the patronage of some great nobleman, whose name it took; but in fact the companies were independent commercial organisations.

In 1594 there was a regrouping of the London theatrical companies after a severe plague, and Shakespeare and seven other actors joined forces to form a new company, the Lord Chamberlain's Men, which rapidly became the leading company of the time, with Richard Burbage as its outstanding performer. In 1599 Shakespeare was one of a consortium of investors who built the famous Globe Theatre, which became the normal home of the Chamberlain's Men. In 1603, when James I came to the throne, he took the company under his own direct patronage, and changed its name to the King's Men. Besides enjoying enormous success with the public, the company was invited more often than any other to perform at court before the sovereign during the Christmas revels and similar festivities, and Shakespeare's plays were frequently performed on these occasions.

As, after 1594, the Lord Chamberlain's Men established themselves as London's leading company, so Shakespeare established himself as its leading playwright. In the early part of his career he wrote about two plays a year, mostly history-plays and comedies, and in these he achieved a brilliant synthesis of the popular, academic, and courtly traditions. After 1600 he wrote about one play a year; these were mainly tragedies, until the very end of his career, when he wrote the so-called romances. In about 1612 he retired from the London theatre and returned to Stratford, where he was now rich enough to buy the best house in the town. He died in 1616.

Shakespeare's history plays

By history plays we mean ones dealing with *English* history. Shakespeare wrote ten of them, and with one exception they were written in the first ten years of his career, 1589-99. The exception is *Henry VIII*, written in collaboration with John Fletcher in about 1613. Of the nine plays from the early part of his career, one stands by itself, namely *King John*. The remaining eight depict one continuous period of English history from the reign of Richard II in the fourteenth century to the accession of Henry VII, the first of the Tudor kings, in 1485. These eight plays are often called Shakespeare's history-cycle.

The four plays depicting the earlier events of the cycle were in fact written second. *Richard II* (c. 1595) shows the deposition and murder of Richard II by his cousin Henry Bolingbroke, Duke of Lancaster, who becomes Henry IV. The two parts of *Henry IV* (c. 1597) show the consequent troubles of Henry IV's reign, as the noblemen who helped him to the throne rebel against him in turn. In *Henry V* (1599), these troubles for the Lancastrian monarchy are temporarily smoothed over as the great warrior-king leads his English army to the conquest of France. But retribution is merely postponed: in the other half of the cycle, the consequences of the original murder and deposition of Richard II come home to roost. The three parts of *Henry VI (c.* 1589-91) begin immediately after the death of Henry V; during the long reign of his son, the English possessions in France are lost, and then civil war breaks out in England, as the Duke of York challenges the Lancastrian right to the throne; after bloody wars and murders, the Yorkists triumph, and Edward IV becomes king. In *Richard III (c.* 1592), the younger brother of Edward IV schemes and murders his way to the throne, but finally this monster-king is overthrown by Henry Richmond, who unites the houses of York and Lancaster by marrying the Yorkist heiress, and inaugurates the Tudor era as Henry VII.

Henry VII had been careful to get the history of these troubles related by chroniclers from his own point of view, and the sources from which Shakespeare drew his material presented the offical Tudor view of history. Inevitably, therefore, Shakespeare also presents this point of view in his cycle: the importance of legitimacy, the horrors of disorder and civil war, the role of the Tudors as bringers of peace and prosperity. Despite this fact, the plays are probing and questioning ones, preoccupied with the problems of the public world—government, war, power, kingship—and with the relationship between the public world and morality. There is a brilliant realism, an observation of men's behaviour in political situations which is blurred neither by sentimentality nor by cynicism. Whatever Shakespeare may have believed about hierarchy, he shows how in practice Richard II's belief in his own divine right is unable to protect him against the folly of his political behaviour; and equally how the strong and efficient man who succeeds him, Henry IV, is unable to bring peace to the country, because of the way he had seized the throne.

A note on the text

In 1623, seven years after Shakespeare's death, some of his former colleagues published his collected plays in one large volume. This was a folio volume, that is, the pages were very large, since they represented half a sheet of paper: each sheet was folded only once in the making of the book. This edition of 1623 is called the Shakespeare First Folio, and is our sole authority for about half the plays. A number of the plays, however, had been published individually during his lifetime, as quarto volumes. A quarto is smaller than a folio, since the page represents only a quarter of a sheet of paper: each sheet is folded twice in the making of the book.

Shakespeare himself seems to have had no interest in publishing his plays. It was against the interests of the company to publish, because there was no law of copyright, and to publish a play was to make a present of it to rival companies. Plays might, however, be published if the company was very short of money, for example during a time of plague (when the theatres were closed), or when a play was getting old. Sometimes a pirated edition of a play appeared: an unscrupulous printer would bribe one or more of the hired actors in a company to reconstruct a play from memory. This is probably what happened with *Henry V*. A quarto edition of it was published in 1600, but is a very corrupt text, with many obvious mistakes and omissions, and it looks like a pirate edition reconstructed by the actors who played the parts of Exeter and Gower. This 'bad quarto' was reprinted in 1602 and 1619. In 1623 an authentic version of the play appeared in the First Folio, and the First Folio (F1) text is the one on which any modern edition must be based, though just occasionally the First Quarto (Q1) can help to correct errors or omissions in F1. It seems likely from internal evidence that the text of *Henry V* in F1 was printed from a version in Shakespeare's own hand, perhaps the manuscript which he submitted to the company, which would have contained few stage-directions and probably no act or scene divisions. There are no scene divisions in the F1 version; there are act divisions, but these are obviously wrong, and are regularly corrected by modern editors; they were presumably inserted by the compilers of F1. The text in F1 is a good one, with few obscurities or corrupt passages, and is well-punctuated. The only passages which contain many errors are those written in French: the compositor setting up the text obviously did not know French, and misread many words. In modern editions, these French passages have undergone a good deal of correction.

Different editions of *Henry V* have somewhat different line-numbers. This is because many of the scenes contain prose, which occupies a different number of lines in different editions. It is therefore necessary to give line-numbers from one particular edition, and for these *Notes* the edition chosen is one of the cheap and easily-available paperback editions, that in the New Penguin Shakespeare:

WILLIAM SHAKESPEARE, *Henry V*, edited by A.R. Humphreys,
  Penguin Books, Harmondsworth, 1968.

If you use a different edition, you should have no difficulty in identifying passages referred to, since the numbering is seldom likely to differ by more than four or five lines.

Part 2

Summaries
of HENRY V

A general summary

Henry V has succeeded to the throne of England. During his father's lifetime, he had been a wild young prince, but is now a reformed character and a model king. He is contemplating an invasion of France, on the grounds that he is the true heir to the French throne, and asks the Archbishop of Canterbury whether this claim is a just one. The Archbishop argues that it is, and that an attack on France by Henry would be a just war. Henry's nobles join the Archbishop in urging him to invade France. Henry decides to undertake the war. Ambassadors arrive from the Dauphin, the son of the King of France, with a contemptuous message; in reply, Henry threatens war. He assembles an army and a fleet at Southampton. Here it is discovered that three of his followers have been bribed by the French to assassinate him; they are arrested and executed. Henry lands in France with his army, and sends ambassadors to the French king demanding the crown; the French king offers Henry the hand of his daughter in marriage, and certain dukedoms, but this offer is rejected. Henry captures the town of Harfleur, and leaves a garrison in it. With his remaining forces, which are much depleted by sickness, he begins to march towards Calais. The French assemble a large army, and intercept him near Agincourt. In the ensuing battle the French, despite a numerical superiority of five to one, are overwhelmingly defeated. Henry returns to England in triumph. Through the mediation of the Duke of Burgundy, a meeting takes place between Henry and the French king, and a treaty is negotiated whereby Henry is to marry Katherine, the French king's daughter, and to be recognised as heir to the French throne. While the final details of the treaty are being settled, there is a scene in which Henry woos Katherine. The play ends with general amity and prayers that war shall never again take place between England and France.

Detailed summaries

Prologue

The Chorus apologises to the audience for the limitations of the theatre and the actors, which cannot do justice to the great historical events depicted in the play. He asks the audience to use their imaginations in order to remedy the deficiencies of the performance.

NOTES AND GLOSSARY:

The Chorus is not a group of speakers, but a single actor. He appears at the beginning of each of the five acts, and adds an epilogue at the end of the play. On the functions of the Chorus, see the specimen essay in Part 4 below (pp 71–3).

Muse of fire: in classical mythology, the Muses were goddesses of learning and the arts, who inspired writers. Of fire, because in traditional theory the natural place of the element fire was above the other three elements

invention: in rhetorical theory, the stage of the creative process in which the writer found suitable material for his work. Here the word must be pronounced as four syllables (*in-vén-si-ón*)

the port of Mars: deportment of Mars, the Roman god of war

gentles: gentlemen and gentlewomen

scaffold: stage

cockpit: the theatre (shaped like the arenas used for cockfighting)

wooden O: the theatre (circular in shape)

a crooked figure: a nought

ciphers to this great accompt: noughts (zeros) compared to this great sum

imaginary forces: powers of imagination

abutting fronts: projecting foreheads. Referring to the high chalk cliffs at Dover and Calais, where England and France are nearest

puissánce: power, armed force. Originally a French word, and pronounced as three syllables (*pú-i-ssánce*)

Turning ... hour-glass: making achievements which took many years into something which occupies a single hour. The events depicted in the play took place in 1414–20

for the which supply: as an aid to which

Act I Scene 1

The Archbishop of Canterbury and the Bishop of Ely discuss a proposal in Parliament which would strip the Church of many of its possessions. To gain the favour of the King, and to block this proposal, Canterbury has offered him a large sum of money from the Church for a war against France. He is going to explain in detail to the King the justice of his claim to the French throne. We also hear about the King's former wildness and his sudden reformation on his father's death.

NOTES AND GLOSSARY:

bill: proposed Act of Parliament

scambling: contentious, violent

lazars: poor and diseased persons, lepers

Consideration: spiritual contemplation

like an angel ... spirits: in the Bible, after the Fall of Man, Adam and Eve were driven out of the Garden of Eden (Paradise) by God (Genesis 3:23–4). The sinful nature of man was called 'the old Adam' in him: so to drive out Adam from the King was to drive out sinfulness. The whole passage indicates that the King's change of behaviour was a religious conversion

Hydra-headed: in classical mythology, the Hydra was a many-headed monster, killed by Hercules. Each time a head was cut off, two more grew in its place

The Gordian knot: a complicated knot tied by a Phrygian king. An oracle prophesied that whoever loosened the knot would rule over all Asia. Alexander the Great cut through it with his sword. The suggestion here is that Henry is superior to Alexander: the latter was skilled only in war, but Henry is also skilled in politics, in which he can actually *untie* the Gordian knot (unravel complicated problems)

a chartered libertine: somebody permitted to wander about at will, like a freeman

His companies: the people he mixed with

sequestration ... popularity: withdrawal from public places and from mixing with the common people

crescive in his faculty: growing by means of its internal powers. The normal possessive form of *it* was *his*; the form *its* was not invented until about 1600, and is very rare in Shakespeare

miracles are ceased: it was held by Protestants (but not by Catholics) that miracles had ceased to occur after the coming of Christ

admit the means: admit the existence of (natural) causes

perfected: stressed on the first syllable

exhibiters: the people introducing the Bill in Parliament

severals and unhidden passages: details and clear lines of descent

seat: throne

Act I Scene 2

The King asks the Archbishop of Canterbury to explain whether or not the Salic Law invalidates his claim to the French throne; he warns the Archbishop not to twist the truth, because a war between England and France will cause great bloodshed. The Archbishop replies that the Salic Law says that no woman shall succeed to an inheritance in Salic territory; but this territory was part of Germany, not of France; and there had been French kings whose claim to the throne passed through a female; Henry's claim to the throne is therefore just. The Archbishop and the King's counsellors urge him to attack France. The King points out the danger that, if England attacks France, the Scots will attack England. They discuss the measures necessary to guard against this, and the Archbishop makes a long speech on the necessity for order and obedience in a society, pointing to the natural order found in a hive of bees. The King makes his decision: he will attack France. The French ambassadors, who have been waiting to see him, are admitted. They bring a message from the Dauphin, rejecting a claim by Henry to certain French dukedoms, and making contemptuous references to Henry's youth and wild life; Henry cannot gain French dukedoms by revelling, and the Dauphin sends him a more suitable gift, a barrel of treasure. The 'treasure', on inspection, is found to be tennis-balls. In a majestic reply, Henry threatens war and vengeance. He orders his followers to prepare for the expedition against France.

NOTES AND GLOSSARY:

we would be resolved ... of some things of weight: I wish to be freed from doubt concerning certain important matters. The King often uses the 'royal plural' (*we* instead of *I*), especially when speaking formally

the law Salic: the Salic Law is a collection of popular laws of the Salic Franks, dating from heathen times. This code, however, says nothing about inheritance through a female. The rule forbidding the inheritance of the French crown through a female was not invented until the fourteenth century; it was probably called the Salic Law to make it sound ancient and respectable

Pharamond: the legendary ancestor of the kings of the Franks

Charles the Great: Charlemagne (742–814), king of the Franks, and later Emperor

the year of our redemption: the date reckoned from the birth of Christ

Conveyed himself as: pretended to be

coursing snatchers: fast-riding robbers

in the Book of Numbers: the biblical passage runs (in the 1611 translation): If a man die, and have no son, then ye shall cause his inheritance to pass unto his daughter (Numbers 27:8). The Archbishop omits the words *and have no son*

your great-grandsire: Henry's great-grandfather, Edward III. At the Battle of Crecy (1346), Edward III's son, the Black Prince, defeated the French. Edward watched the battle from a hill with one-third of the English forces, who were held in reserve and never used

the main intendment: the intention (of attacking us) with a large army. A *main* army was a large and fully-equipped one, as contrasted with small raiding-parties

impounded as a stray: locked up, as straying cattle are locked up in a village cattle-pen

the King of Scots: David II, captured by the English in 1346 while Edward III was away in France

For government . . . close: the image is from music. In a well-ordered state, people of different ranks (*high, and low, and lower*) are like the *parts* (different melodic lines) in music, which keep in harmony (*consent*) with one another, and co-operate (*congree*) to produce a cadence (*close*) at the end of the musical phrase

a king (line 190): in fact a queen, but Shakespeare is following traditional belief as found in classical writers

of sorts: of various ranks

mechanic: belonging to the class of manual labourers who work in a trade

executors: executioners

dial: sundial

Gallia: France

worried: harassed, seized by the throat (by a dog)

hardiness and policy: boldness and statesmanship

resolved: both 'freed from doubt' and 'determined on a course of action'. Henry has now decided on the war with France, and so sends for the French ambassadors who are waiting to see him

mute: a house-servant whose tongue had been removed to make him dumb

waxen: perishable, short-lived

May't please . . . embassy: the Dauphin's message is so rude that the ambassadors will not deliver it without first getting Henry's permission to tell it bluntly

galliard: a quick and lively dance

When we have matched ... chases:	Henry uses technical terms from tennis, often with a double meaning. This was not the modern game of lawn-tennis, but the earlier game played in an enclosed court. A *hazard* was a hole in the wall of the court: a player who struck the ball into a hazard won a point. The *chase* was the second bounce of the ball on the floor. Notice also *set, match, courts,* and *crown* (the coin usually staked on a game, with a pun on the king's crown)
keep my state:	observe the pomp and ceremony befitting my rank
rise ... dazzle:	like the sun, a common symbol for royalty
gun-stones:	cannon-balls
proportions:	forces

Act II Chorus

The young men of England prepare enthusiastically for the war. The French are frightened, and bribe three high-placed Englishmen to kill the King in Southampton, where he intends to embark his army. The scene will move to Southampton, whence the actors will carry the audience safely to France and back.

NOTES AND GLOSSARY:

silken dalliance ... lies:	the young men have discarded the silk clothes suitable for frivolous behaviour or flirtation
Mercuries:	the Roman god Mercury was depicted as a young man with winged sandals and a winged hat
hollow bosoms:	(*a*) insincere hearts (*b*) empty pockets
force a play:	impose dramatic form on the historical events
offend one stomach:	(*a*) make anybody sea-sick, (*b*) offend anybody's taste or inclinations

---

Act II Scene 1

Bardolph, Pistol, and Nym, three former companions of the King, are going to the wars. Pistol and Nym have quarrelled, because Pistol has married Hostess Quickly, who had been engaged to Nym. When Pistol and his new wife enter, Nym and Pistol bluster at one another, but both are too cowardly to fight. The Boy, a servant of Sir John Falstaff, brings the news that Falstaff is ill; the Boy and the Hostess go off to see him. Nym and Pistol again bluster, but finally a peace is patched up. The Hostess returns to say that Falstaff's illness is serious, and they all go off to see him, agreeing that the King's treatment of him is one cause of his bad plight.

NOTES AND GLOSSARY:
The Chorus has led us to expect a scene in Southampton, but this scene must be set in London (see the opening of Act II, Scene 3).

Nym:	the name is from the verb *to nim* 'to steal, pilfer'. Nym, Bardolph, and Pistol are thieving rogues
Ancient:	ensign, an army officer one rank below lieutenant
wink:	close both eyes (not, as today, one eye)
iron:	sword
rest:	final determination
rendezvous:	refuge, last resort
Nell Quickly:	later referred to as *Hostess* or *Hostess Quickly*. In the *Henry IV* plays she was hostess (landlady) of a London tavern frequented by Prince Hal and Falstaff
troth-plight:	formally betrothed, engaged
straight:	immediately
shog off:	go away (*slang*)
solus:	alone (*Latin*)
take:	strike, catch fire
cock:	the hammer or striking-lever of a fire-arm. Pistol is punning on his own name
Barbason:	the name of a devil
conjure:	control a devil or spirit by means of a spell. Nym means that Pistol cannot influence him merely by words
humour:	inclination
that's the humour of it:	a modish expression of the time, here meaning 'that's how I feel', or 'that's the situation'
mickle:	great
tall:	brave
in fair terms:	another fashionable cliché, meaning 'to express it politely'; but Nym apparently uses it to mean 'thoroughly'
Couple a gorge:	Pistol's attempt at the French *couper la gorge* 'cut the throat'
spital:	hospital, especially one for the poor and for people with foul diseases (such as leprosy, venereal disease)
powdering tub:	the sweating-tub used in the treatment of venereal disease
lazar kite of Cressid's kind:	diseased bird of prey of Cressida's sort (a whore)
Doll Tearsheet:	a prostitute who appears in *Henry IV Part 2*, where she is entertained by Falstaff

quondam:	former (*Latin*). No longer Quickly, because she has married
the only she:	the only woman
pauca:	for *pauca verba* (*Latin*) 'few words'
my master:	Falstaff
thy face:	Bardolph's face and nose are extremely red, a subject for frequent jokes

yield the crow a pudding: provide a meal for the crows, that is, to die (*proverbial*)

the King has killed his heart: on becoming king, Henry had publicly renounced Falstaff and his other cronies. The Hostess suggests that Falstaff will die of a broken heart

As manhood shall compound: as real men settle such debts (by fighting, not paying)

an thou wilt:	if you will
noble:	a gold coin worth six shillings and eightpence. Pistol offers Nym immediate payment of rather less than he owes him, and drinks
sutler:	one who sells provisions to the army
quotidian tertian:	the word *fever* is understood. But the Hostess misuses these big words: a quotidian fever was one where attacks occurred every day, whereas in a tertian fever they occurred every other day

run bad humours on: caused to be melancholy

the even:	the plain truth

fracted and corroborate: a pompous way of saying 'broken'; but in fact *corroborate* meant 'strengthened'

careers:	a technical term of horsemanship. A career was a short gallop at full speed, or a charge, or the quick turning of a horse from side to side

---

Act II Scene 2

Southampton. We learn that some traitors have been detected but not yet arrested. The King enters with Scroop, Cambridge, and Grey, and asks their opinions on the prospects for the war. He orders that a man imprisoned for speaking against him shall be pardoned and freed; the three oppose this, as being too lenient. The King gives them their commissions, but when they open them they find the evidence of their treason; they kneel and ask for mercy. The King points out that they themselves have just argued against mercy, and are condemned out of their own mouths. He reproaches them for their unnaturalness and ingratitude, and grieves at their corruption. They express repentance, and ask the King's personal forgiveness. He sentences them to death, and they are taken away. The King orders the army to put to sea.

NOTES AND GLOSSARY:

in head:	as an army
Enlarge:	set free
security:	over-confidence
his sufferance:	indulgence towards him
correction:	punishment
on distemper:	from a disordered condition of the body or mind
late:	recently appointed
ask for it:	ask for the commission: an authority to act for the King in his absence from the country
quick:	alive
By your own counsel:	Henry unfairly disregards the psychology of the situation: the secret traitor will try to appear extremely loyal
Working ... whoop at them:	acting so obviously for a purpose natural to them that no outcry of surprise was caused
voice:	vote
suggest:	tempt, lead astray
he that tempered ... stand up:	the devil that worked on you commanded you to rebel
Tartar:	Tartarus (the hell of classical mythology)
jealousy:	suspicion
affiance:	faith, trust
complement:	personal accomplishments or qualities
bolted:	sifted; hence fine, of choice quality
fall of man:	(see p. 8 in Part 1 above)
discovered:	revealed
earnest:	part-payment made in advance
dear:	serious, grievous
rub:	obstacle
The signs of war advance:	raise the banners

Act II Scene 3

Nym, Bardolph, Pistol, and the Boy are setting off from London for the war. From them and the Hostess we learn that Falstaff has died. They make their farewells to the Hostess, and leave.

NOTES AND GLOSSARY:

bring:	accompany
Staines:	a town about twenty miles west of London
earn:	grieve

Arthur's bosom:	the Hostess means Abraham's bosom, heaven (see the Bible, Luke 16:22), but she confuses Abraham with the legendary British king, Arthur
'A:	he
an (line 11):	as if
christom child:	the Hostess confuses *christen* 'christian' and *chrisom* 'the white cloth put on a child at baptism'. A chrisom-child (one wearing a chrisom) would be very young and innocent
cried out of sack:	cried out against wine
carnation:	the Hostess misunderstands *incarnate* 'in human form', confusing it with *carnation* 'pink, flesh-coloured'
the Whore of Babylon:	an abusive expression used by Protestants to describe the Pope
the fuel:	the liquor that Falstaff bought for Bardolph, which made his nose red
Let senses rule:	be alert
Pitch and pay:	cash only, no credit
wafer-cakes:	a kind of very thin cake, easily broken
Caveto:	be wary (*Latin*)
clear thy crystals:	dry your eyes
housewifery:	thrift, careful housekeeping
Keep close:	remain concealed, stay indoors

Act II Scene 4

The French king, alarmed at the coming English attack, orders defences to be prepared. The Dauphin thinks that the attack is not serious, since the English king is so foolish, but he is contradicted by the Constable and by the King. The Duke of Exeter arrives with a message from Henry, demanding the French crown; he also has a contemptuous message for the Dauphin. The French king promises to reply the following day; Exeter urges haste, since Henry has already landed in France.

NOTES AND GLOSSARY:

line:	strengthen
gulf:	whirlpool
morris-dance:	popular ritual dance performed by teams of men at festivals, especially Whitsuntide
humorous:	capricious, whimsical
Constable:	the Constable of France was head of the royal household, and commander-in-chief of the army

in exception:	in disagreeing, in expressing objections
vanities forespent:	past frivolity
Brutus:	Lucius Junius Brutus helped to free Rome from the Tarquins (510 BC). He had survived the Tarquin tyranny by pretending to be an idiot; hence his name Brutus ('stupid')
fleshed:	To flesh a hawk or hound was to give it part of the prey that had been killed, so that the taste of blood would make it more eager in the chase
present:	immediate
Turn head:	turn and face the pursuing hounds
spend their mouths:	bark
sinister nor awkward:	dishonest or perverse
line:	genealogy, pedigree
evenly derived:	directly descended
Jove:	in classical mythology, Jove (or Jupiter) was the principal god, and wielded the thunderbolt
requiring:	requesting
in the bowels of the Lord:	in the name of God's compassion
second accent:	echo
ordinance:	artillery
Paris balls:	tennis-balls
Louvre:	the palace of the French kings. Probably with a pun on *lover*, which was often pronounced with a long /uː/

Act III Chorus

The Chorus describes the sailing of the English fleet from Southampton. The English army besieges Harfleur. The ambassador returns with an offer from the French king: the hand of his daughter Katherine, with some dukedoms as dowry. The offer is rejected, and the English cannon bombard Harfleur.

NOTES AND GLOSSARY:

imagined wing:	the wings of imagination
brave:	splendid (especially in appearance)
the young Phoebus:	the morning sun. Phoebus was the Roman sun-god
bottoms:	ships
rivage:	shore
Harfleur:	stressed on the first syllable
likes:	pleases
linstock:	a lighted match on a staff, for firing cannon
chambers:	small cannon

Act III Scene 1

The English are trying to storm Harfleur, through a breach made in the walls by their artillery. Henry urges them on.

NOTES AND GLOSSARY:

aspect: stressed on the second syllable
portage: port-holes, openings
galled: worn, beaten (by the waves)
jutty his confounded base: project beyond its worn-away base
fet: inherited
argument: opposition
of grosser blood: not of gentle birth. Henry is addressing the gentlemen and noblemen, who must be an example (*copy*) to the lower ranks. In line 25, he turns to the yeomen—men who were substantial farmers, but below the rank of gentleman
slips: leashes. In hare-coursing, greyhounds raced one another in pursuit of a hare; until the hare was *afoot*, the hounds were held back on leashes
charge ... George: an exact rhyme, *George* being pronounced *Jarge*. St George was the patron saint of England

Act III Scene 2

Harfleur. Bardolph urges his reluctant companions forward to the breach. Fluellen arrives and drives them forward, leaving only the Boy, who soliloquises on the characters of Bardolph, Nym, and Pistol. Four captains—Fluellen (Welsh), Gower (English), Macmorris (Irish), and Jamy (Scots)—discuss the siege. Fluellen attempts to argue with Macmorris about military theory, and they nearly quarrel. A trumpet-call from Harfleur asks for a parley.

NOTES AND GLOSSARY:
Fluellen's pronunciation is shown by spellings like *athversary* 'adversary', *Cheshu* 'Jesu', *plow* 'blow', and *falorous* 'valorous'. His un-English grammar is seen in *He has no more directions ... than is a puppy-dog*. He constantly says *look you*, and loves fine classical words like *concavities* and *pristine*.

the very plainsong: the simple truth
cullions: rascals
bawcock, chuck: familiar terms of endearment
swashers: braggarts, ruffians

antics:	clowns
white-livered:	cowardly
'a breaks words:	(a) he breaks promises, (b) he exchanges words
carry coals:	submit to insult; do dirty or degrading work
pocketing up of wrongs:	(a) putting up with insult or injury, (b) putting stolen goods in my pocket
goes against my ... stomach:	is contrary to my natural inclination
cast:	vomit
presently:	immediately
gud-day:	good day (Scots). Other Scots forms used by Jamy are *sall* 'shall', *vary* 'very', *bath* 'both', *mess* 'mass', *ay* 'I', *lig* 'lie', *grund* 'ground', *wad* 'would', and *tway* 'two'
Chrish:	Christ. Spellings with *sh* for *s* are the main mark of Macmorris's Irish pronunciation, e.g. *ish* 'is'. Notice also *beseeched* 'besieged' and *sa'* 'save'
quit:	repay
breff:	short
Of my nation:	Macmorris is very touchy about his nationality, and explodes before anything has been said about it

---

Act III Scene 3

Henry gives the Governor of Harfleur a final chance to surrender: otherwise he will storm the town and destroy it. He draws a vivid picture of the murders, rapes, and looting that will occur when the city is sacked. The Governor replies that the military help expected from the Dauphin has not come, and that he therefore surrenders the town, which is no longer defensible. Henry orders Exeter to hold Harfleur against the French; he himself will retreat to Calais, since sickness is spreading among his troops and winter is coming on.

NOTES AND GLOSSARY:

fleshed:	see page 29
fell:	fierce, cruel
bootless:	uselessly, vainly
leviathan:	whale
wives of Jewry ... slaughtermen:	a reference to the biblical story of the Massacre of the Innocents (Matthew 2:16-18). In an attempt to kill the infant Christ, King Herod ordered the killing of all children up to the age of two years in Bethlehem and its neighbourhood
Returns us:	sends us the reply
addressed:	prepared

Act III Scene 4

Katherine, daughter of the French king, is given an elementary English lesson by an old gentlewoman, Alice.

NOTES AND GLOSSARY:
Many of the original audience were unable to understand French; but all the objects named in the scene can be indicated by gestures, so it would quickly become apparent to them that an English lesson was being given; and they could then enjoy its inadequacies. Alice's English is poor: she cannot pronounce *th*, saying *de* for *the*, and she says *nick* and *count* for *neck* and *gown*. Her pupil is worse: *arm, chin,* and *elbow* become *arma, sin,* and *bilbow* (a bar fastened to the legs of prisoners). For those in the audience who could understand French, there was the additional comedy of Alice's sycophancy: she assures the princess that she pronounces English as well as a native speaker, and praises her for the acquisition of nine English words. Some of their pronunciations, moreover, produce obscenities, on two of which Katherine comments.

Act III Scene 5

The French king and his nobility express their chagrin that the English have marched so far through France without opposition. The King orders a large force to march against Henry and take him prisoner. The Constable regrets that the English army is so small and enfeebled: when Henry sees the French army, he will surrender. The King sends the herald Montjoy to Henry, to negotiate his ransom.

NOTES AND GLOSSARY:

Somme: the crossing of the Somme was halfway along Henry's route from Harfleur to Calais, a journey of about 170 miles

sprays ... grafters: the metaphor is from the gardener's technique of grafting: shoots (*sprays*) of a plant are inserted in another *stock*, and are then called *scions*. The Dauphin means that the English are merely illegitimate descendants of the Frenchmen who seized England at the Norman Conquest

luxury: lust

nook-shotten: having many corners. Referring contemptuously to the shape of England (*Albion*)

sodden water ... barley broth: beer, despised by the wine-drinking French

sur-reined jades: overworked horses

Decoct: make warm
poor we call them in their native lords: we say the fields are poor with
          respect to the French lords who own them
lavoltas, corantos: two lively dances. The French are fit only to be
          dancing-masters, not warriors

Act III Scene 6

Fluellen has been in action under the Duke of Exeter at a bridge, where
Pistol has been present; Fluellen believes that Pistol is a gallant fighter.
Pistol asks him to intercede with Exeter for Bardolph, who has been
sentenced to death for robbing a church; Fluellen refuses; Pistol takes
offence, and goes. Gower explains to Fluellen what kind of man Pistol
is. The King enters, and Fluellen reports on the situation at the bridge.
The French herald Montjoy brings a message demanding Henry's
surrender and ransom. In reply, Henry admits that his army is small
and weakened by sickness, but refuses to surrender; his army will
continue its march, and will fight if the French try to stop it. The
English army marches on towards the bridge.

NOTES AND GLOSSARY:

the bridge: over the River Ternoise, about sixty miles from
          Calais. Henry rightly feared that the French would
          try to destroy it, and sent a small force on ahead
          to seize it. Fluellen is now returning to report the
          successful capture of the bridge
Agamemnon: King of Mycenae, and commander of the Greek
          army at the siege of Troy
Mark Antony: Marcus Antonius (*c.* 82–30 BC), an outstanding
          Roman general
buxom: vigorous
Fortune: Fortune (the Roman goddess Fortuna) was a com-
          mon theme in Renaissance literature and art. She
          was depicted as a female figure, turning a wheel on
          which men rise and fall, or balancing blindfold on
          a rolling stone
mutability, and variation: mutable and varying. Fluellen is
          ungrammatical
vital thread: The three Fates (the Roman Parcae) wove the web
          of a man's life; when the third of them cut the web,
          the man's life ended
figo: Spanish for 'fig', used as a term of contempt, often
          accompanied by an obscene gesture
sconce: small fort or earthwork

find a hole in his coat: find him at fault
passages: fighting
was have: had. More un-English grammar
bubukles: Fluellen confuses *bubo* and *carbuncle*, both names for inflamed swellings on the human body
tucket: trumpet-call
habit: clothing. Heralds wore a distinctive uniform
bruise an injury: squeeze a boil or abscess
sufferance: self-restraint
quality: profession, rank
impeachment: opposition
craft and vantage: superior strength
worthless trunk: his own body

Act III Scene 7

The camp of the French army, less than a mile from the English. It is night, and a battle will be fought in the morning. The French nobility are impatient for the dawn, when they will ride over the English dead and each will have a hundred prisoners.

NOTES AND GLOSSARY:
I will not change ... pasterns: he would only exchange it for a flying horse. The pastern is the lower part of a horse's leg
as if his entrails were hairs: like a tennis ball. Tennis-balls were stuffed with hair
Pegasus: a winged horse of Greek mythology
Hermes: a Greek god. He invented the lyre and the reed-pipe, on which he played ravishing music
Perseus: a hero of Greek mythology. He had a pair of winged sandals with which he could fly
argument: subject
prescript: prescribed, proper
kern: Irish foot-soldier or peasant
straight strossers: tight trousers. Trousers were worn by the Irish, but not by the English, who regarded them as barbarous. The Dauphin, continuing the pun on horse and mistress, means that the Constable had nothing on his legs but the skin—his lower parts were naked
jade: (*a*) inferior kind of horse, (*b*) term of contempt for a woman
go to hazard: gamble with dice
go yourself to hazard: put yourself in danger (in battle)
never ... lackey: because the Dauphin has never beaten anybody else

hooded ... bate:	a metaphor from falconry. A leather hood was placed over the head of a hawk when it was not pursuing game. When the hood was removed, the hawk would *bate* (beat its wings impatiently). The Constable is punning on another meaning of *bate* (diminish, become less): when the Dauphin's courage is put to the test, it will shrink away
overshot:	(*a*) wide of the mark, mistaken, (*b*) intoxicated
mope:	wander aimlessly about
fat-brained:	stupid
apprehension:	understanding, intelligence
sympathise with:	resemble
coming on:	attacking
stomachs:	inclinations

Act IV Chorus

The Chorus describes the camps of the two armies by night—the firelight, the sentries, the noises. The French wait impatiently for dawn, playing at dice; the English sit seriously by their fires contemplating their peril. Henry goes round the camp, encouraging his soldiers, and raising morale by his own calm and cheerfulness. The Chorus apologises for the inadequacy of the representation of the Battle of Agincourt which is to follow.

NOTES AND GLOSSARY:

poring:	making the eyes tired
battle:	army
umbered:	made a yellow-brown colour (by the firelight)
accomplishing:	completing the arming of
secure:	carefree, over-confident
play:	stake as wagers
Captain:	general, commander-in-chief
overbears attaint:	overcomes the effect on his appearance
mean:	plebeian
gentle:	of high birth
as may unworthiness define:	in so far as our inadequate theatre can represent it
foils:	swordsmen. A foil was a blunted sword used in fencing
Agincourt:	the village (now called *Azincourt*) near which the ensuing battle took place, about halfway between Calais and Amiens
mockeries:	imitations (representations on the stage)

Act IV Scene 1

The English camp, shortly before dawn. Henry borrows a cloak to disguise himself, and goes around incognito. He encounters Pistol, and overhears Fluellen and Gower. He meets three ordinary soldiers, Bates, Court, and Williams, and argues with them about the situation of the army and the responsibility of the King. Henry and Williams quarrel; they exchange gloves as gages, to be worn in their caps after the battle; Williams undertakes to challenge the wearer of his glove, and give him a box on the ear. In a soliloquy, Henry meditates on the hard lot of a king: he has great responsibility and no rest, and his only advantage over ordinary men is ceremony, which is worthless. Erpingham arrives to say that Henry's nobles are hunting for him; he sends Erpingham to collect them at his tent. In a prayer, Henry asks God to give his soldiers courage, and not to punish him for his father's seizure of the crown. Gloucester arrives, and they leave for Henry's tent.

NOTES AND GLOSSARY:

dress us: prepare ourselves

With casted slough: like a snake which has cast its skin

God-a-mercy: God reward you

gentleman of a company: person of gentle rank who served voluntarily as an ordinary soldier

imp: young shoot of a plant; child

bully: good fellow

le Roy: French for 'the King'

St Davy's day: March 1st. St David was the patron saint of Wales, and on his day Welshmen wore leeks in their caps

admiration: astonishing thing

Pompey the Great: Gnaeus Pompeius (106-48 BC), a famous Roman general

tiddle-taddle ... pibble-pabble: Fluellen's pronunciations of *tittle-tattle* and *bibble-babble*, 'idle chatter, excessive talking'

element shows: sky appears

stoop: descend. A hawk was said to stoop when it swooped on its prey

at all adventures: whatever the risk, at all costs

so we were quit here: provided we were out of this situation

latter day: Last Judgement

rawly: very young

against all proportion of subjection: in complete violation of the proper relationship between ruler and subject

beadle: minor local official, whose duties included whipping certain offenders

You pay him then:	that will be terrible for him, won't it!
elder-gun:	pop-gun (a child's toy)
round:	rude, blunt
enow:	enough
cut ... crowns:	(*a*) clip pieces off coins, (*b*) cut people's heads
wringing:	physical pain
comings-in:	income
blown from adulation:	inflated by flattery
balm:	holy oil poured on the King's head at his coronation
farced:	inflated, pompous
distressful:	gained by painful labour
Phoebus:	the sun
Elysium:	the heaven of classical mythology; hence, a state of ideal happiness
Hyperion:	the Greek sun-god. The slave is up at dawn
wots:	knows, understands
watch:	wakefulness
Whose hours ... advantages:	whose hours of wakefulness do most benefit to the peasant. *Advantages* is a verb
jealous of:	anxious about
Richard's body:	Richard II had been deposed and murdered by Henry's father, Henry IV
chantries:	chapels where priests said daily prayers for the souls of particular dead people

Act IV Scene 2

The French camp, early morning. The French nobles are eager for battle. The Constable makes a speech of encouragement, saying how little there is for them to do. Grandpré describes the sorry plight of the English army. They leave for the attack.

NOTES AND GLOSSARY:

Via:	an exclamation of encouragement—Come on!
dout:	put out
shales:	shells
hilding:	worthless, contemptible
Took ... speculation:	stood and looked idly on
tucket sonance:	trumpet-call
dare:	daze, paralyse with fear. Larks were dared (terrified from rising) by fowlers, and then netted on the ground. The English, similarly, will be overawed and will tamely surrender

carrions:	corpses
curtains:	banners
Mars:	the Roman god of war
beaver:	moveable face-guard on a helmet
Lob:	hang, droop
gimmaled:	hinged, jointed
battle:	army
trumpet:	trumpeter

Act IV Scene 3

The English camp, early morning. The English nobility contemplate the fearful odds they are facing. Westmorland wishes that they had ten thousand men from England, but Henry rejects this wish. In a speech of encouragement, he says that any soldier in the army who wishes may leave; he then looks forward to the time when the day of this battle will be celebrated yearly in England, and the names of all who fought there will be household words. Salisbury announces that the French are about to attack. Montjoy again comes and demands ransom; Henry again refuses. The Duke of York asks for the privilege of leading the vanguard, which he is granted. They leave for the battle.

NOTES AND GLOSSARY:

honour:	military glory
yearns:	grieves
the best hope I have:	his salvation, heaven
Feast of Crispian:	the festival of St Crispinus and St Crispianus, 25 October
with advantages:	with additions and exaggerations. A humorous touch
expedience:	speed
compound:	agree, come to terms
The man ... hunting him:	A well-known story, based on Æsop's fable about the hunter and the bear. Here a lion is more appropriate than a bear, since the lion is a symbol of royalty
in brass:	in the form of epitaphs on brass memorials
Killing ... mortality:	killing while they are themselves decaying in death
They'll be in fresher ... service:	either they will be in fresh clothes in heaven, or they will have new clothes on earth by taking them from the defeated French
vaward:	vanguard

Act IV Scene 4

The field of battle. A French soldier has surrendered to Pistol, but the Frenchman speaks no English, and Pistol no French. With the aid of the Boy as interpreter, Pistol spares the life of the Frenchman for a ransom of two hundred crowns. The Boy soliloquises on the emptiness of Pistol, and also reveals that the English baggage is defended only by boys.

NOTES AND GLOSSARY:

In considering Pistol's misunderstandings of what the Frenchman says, remember that both English and French have changed in pronunciation since the sixteenth century. The French word *Dieu* was probably pronounced very similarly to English *dew*; and the French word *bras* and the English *brass* had almost identical pronunciations.

Alarums:	loud noises of fighting, gunfire, calls to arms, warning sounds
Excursions:	sorties, groups of soldiers passing over the stage
Calitie ... custure me:	Pistol cannot understand what the Frenchman says, so replies with some nonsense of his own. *Calen o Custure me* was the refrain of a well-known song; originally it was probably Irish, but to the Elizabethans it was just a nonsense-refrain
Perpend:	consider
fox:	sword
Egregious:	very large
Moy:	French for 'me', but Pistol takes it to be the name of a coin
luxurious:	lecherous
fer:	a meaningless verb formed from the name *Fer*
firk:	beat, whip
ferret:	hunt, worry

Owy, cuppele gorge, permafoy: Pistol's attempt at *Oui, couper la gorge, par ma foi*

roaring devil i'th'old play: in the popular religious plays of the late Middle Ages, devils had become comic characters; there were plays in which a devil was beaten with a wooden dagger and made to roar, or had his nails pared with one

that everyone may pare his nails: whose nails anyone may pare

might have a good prey: as indeed happens: see IV.7.1. The Boy is presumably killed in this incident

Act IV Scene 5

The battle-field. The French ranks have been broken, and the French nobility express their shame. There are still enough Frenchmen in the field to win by sheer numbers, if only there were any order, but all is confusion. The noblemen throw themselves back into the battle, in order to die rather than survive in such shame.

NOTES AND GLOSSARY:

confounded:	ruined, lost
perdurable:	everlasting. Stressed on the first and third syllables
gentler:	of higher social class

Act IV Scene 6

The battle-field. Henry praises his soldiers, but warns them that there is still more to do: the French are still in the field. Exeter describes the deaths of the Duke of York and the Earl of Suffolk. There is an alarum: the French are regrouping. Henry orders his soldiers to kill their prisoners.

NOTES AND GLOSSARY:

Larding:	enriching (with his blood)
honour-owing:	possessing honour, honourable
haggled:	mangled, hacked
raught:	reached
my mother:	the tender qualities inherited from my mother
compound:	come to terms
kill his prisoners:	the killing of the prisoners is shown as a military necessity, as in Shakespeare's sources

Act IV Scene 7

The battle-field. Fluellen and Gower are indignant because fleeing French troops have pillaged the King's tent and killed the boys guarding the baggage. Fluellen praises Henry in a long comparison with Alexander the Great. Henry enters with his train and prisoners; he sends a message to a body of French horse on a hill, threatening to kill his prisoners unless they either leave the field or come down and fight. The French herald comes to concede that the French are defeated, and to ask permission for the dead to be buried; Henry sends English heralds with him to catalogue the dead on both sides. Henry sees Williams with the glove in his cap, and questions him about it; he sends him with a message to Gower. He then gives Williams's glove to Fluellen, telling him to wear it in his cap: if anybody challenges it, he must be arrested as a traitor; he sends Fluellen with a message to Gower. He sends Warwick and Gloucester after Fluellen, to prevent any injury when Williams and Fluellen meet.

NOTES AND GLOSSARY:
We again see the peculiarities of Fluellen's English. He replaces /b/ by /p/, as in *poys, porn, Pig, prains, gipes, prave, plood, pless*; notice also *offert* 'offered', *'orld* 'world', *sall* 'shall', *Tavy* 'Davy', *aggriefed* 'aggrieved'. He sometimes uses a plural noun instead of a singular, as in *one reckonings, tales, majesties*; and sometimes the plural form of a verb instead of the singular, as in *know*. He confuses different parts of speech: in *a little variations* he uses a noun instead of a past participle or adjective; and in *is good knowledge and literatured* there is complete grammatical confusion.

Monmouth: the town on the Welsh borders where Henry V was born (1387).

Alexander the Great: Alexander (356-323 BC) was King of Macedon, and conquered large parts of Asia. He was one of the heroes of the Renaissance, and is a frequent source of literary references and comparisons

variations: varied

is come after: has followed, resembled

Cleitus: Alexander's foster-brother, and one of his generals. Alexander killed him in a drunken quarrel

great-belly doublet: a doublet was a close-fitting garment for the upper part of the body. A great-belly doublet was one with the lower part stuffed so that it stood out. A reference to Falstaff's notorious fatness

fined: fixed as the amount to be paid

book: list, record

Yerk: lash, strike

Monmouth caps: flat round caps formerly worn by soldiers and sailors

I am Welsh: See note on *Monmouth* above

Wye: a river which flows through Monmouth and into the Severn

quite from the answer of his degree: free from the necessity of accepting a challenge from a man of Williams's social class

Call him hither: Gower was on stage earlier in the scene, and must have gone off at some point after line 52

this favour: Williams's glove

Alençon: the Duke of Alencon, who was killed in the battle

go seek him: Henry sends both Williams and Fluellen to find Gower, thus making sure that they will meet

Act IV Scene 8

Williams has found Gower and delivered the King's message. Fluellen arrives with the same message. Williams recognises his glove in Fluellen's cap, and strikes him. Fluellen accuses Williams of treason, but Warwick and Gloucester arrive before a brawl can begin. Henry arrives, and Fluellen denounces Williams. Williams produces his own glove and shows that it is the fellow to the one in Fluellen's cap. Henry in turn produces the fellow to the glove in Williams's cap, and reveals that it was he with whom Williams had quarrelled. Williams makes a dignified apologia for his own conduct; the King accepts it, and rewards Williams by filling his glove with crowns. An English herald brings a list of the dead: the French have suffered appalling losses, the English hardly any. Henry commands that there is to be no boasting about the victory: all the credit is to be given to God.

NOTES AND GLOSSARY:

forsworn: Williams had sworn to strike the man who wore his glove. Fluellen himself had argued that Williams ought to keep his oath (IV.7.130-39)

plows: blows

My liege . . . conscience, now: When Fluellen gets excited, his English grammar becomes even worse than usual: *is take* 'took', *hear* 'hears', *is pear* 'will bear', *will avouchment* 'will avouch', *is give* 'gave'.

All offences . . . pardon me: Williams's defence of himself is unanswerable; Henry tacitly acknowledges this in his response

honour: mark of distinction

Non Nobis and Te Deum: The *Non Nobis* is Psalm 115, beginning (in the 1611 English version) 'Not unto us, O Lord, not unto us, but unto thy name give glory'. The *Te Deum* is an old Latin hymn of thanksgiving, beginning (in the English prayer-book version) 'We praise thee, O God, we acknowledge thee to be the Lord'

Act V Chorus

After Agincourt, Henry goes to Calais, and then returns to England, where he is given a triumphal welcome. The Emperor visits England on behalf of France, to try to arrange a peace. Henry returns to France.

NOTES AND GLOSSARY:

pales in: encloses (like a fence)

flood: sea

whiffler:	armed attendant who keeps the way clear for a procession
Blackheath:	an open space just outside London, on the road from Dover (where Henry had landed)
In the quick . . . thought:	in imagination. The forge suggests the power of the mind to shape things to its desire, as the smith shapes the glowing iron by hammering it
working house:	workshop
his brethren:	the aldermen of the city of London, from whose number the Lord Mayor was chosen
Caesar:	a name adopted as a title by the Roman Emperors
a lower but loving likelihood:	a likely event which is less exalted but much desired
the General:	Robert Devereux, second Earl of Essex (1566-1601). In 1599, Queen Elizabeth ('our gracious Empress') sent him to Ireland as Governor-General, to suppress a rebellion
broached:	impaled
The Emperor:	of the Holy Roman Empire. The Emperor Sigismund visited England in 1416
remembering:	reminding
brook:	tolerate

Act V Scene 1

Fluellen is still wearing a leek in his cap, although St David's day is past. He explains to Gower that Pistol has mocked his leek, and he is going to teach him a lesson. Pistol enters, and Fluellen beats him with a cudgel and makes him eat the leek. Gower reproaches Pistol for his malice and cowardice. Left alone, Pistol decides to return to England and live as a pimp and pickpocket, and to pretend that the wounds that Fluellen has given him are war-wounds.

NOTES AND GLOSSARY:

ass:	as
yesterday:	obviously St David's day: see note to Act IV Scene 1 above
swelling like a turkey-cock:	this vividly suggests Pistol's appearance—puffing out his chest and walking with a strut
bedlam:	mad
Troyan:	Trojan; here obviously a term of abuse
fold up Parca's fatal web:	kill you. See note to Act III, Scene 6 above

Cadwallader:	Cadwaladr ap Cadwallon ap Cadfan, a prince of Gwynedd (North Wales) who died in AD 664. In later centuries he became a legendary figure, and there were prophecies that he would return to defeat and expel the English
goats:	a contemptuous reference to the fact that Wales was mountainous and relatively poor
squire of low degree:	the name of a medieval romance, here used jokingly
green:	fresh
coxcomb:	a cap worn by a professional fool or jester, hence the head of a fool
groat:	a coin worth fourpence. Pistol pretends to be insulted by this offer
gleeking and galling:	gibing and scoffing
housewife:	hussy. Fortune is fickle, like a light woman
Doll:	Doll Tearsheet, a whore who appears in *Henry IV Part 2*. But there she is Falstaff's woman, not Pistol's, and Pistol is married to Nell Quickly; so some editors here emend *Doll* to *Nell*
malady of France:	venereal disease
rendezvous:	refuge, place to retire to
scars ... wars:	an exact rhyme in Shakespeare's time
Gallia:	French

Act V Scene 2

The French and English kings and their courts meet to finalise a peace-treaty. The Duke of Burgundy, who has been mediating, describes the decay of civilisation in France because of the war, and urges the desirability of peace. Henry insists on an acceptance of the English demands. The French king asks for a working-party to negotiate the details of the treaty, and this is agreed. Katherine, whose marriage to Henry is one of the English demands, is left with him. He woos her, but disclaims all pretensions to eloquence or courtliness: he is a plain soldier, who can merely say that he loves her. Katherine finally says that, if her father agrees to the marriage, she will be content. The others return, and there is some bantering. It is announced that all the English demands have been accepted, including the marriage and the recognition of Henry as heir to the French throne. There are expressions of general amity, and of wishes that England and France may never again be enemies in war.

NOTES AND GLOSSARY:
balls:	(*a*) eyeballs, (*b*) cannon-balls

basilisks:	(*a*) fabulous reptiles that killed by their look, (*b*) large brass cannon
congreeted:	greeted one another
rub:	obstacle
husbandry:	agricultural produce
it own fertility:	its own fertility
even-pleached:	with branches neatly interlaced
leas:	arable land which has been left untilled

darnel, hemlock ... fumitory: wild plants which flourish in cultivated land

deracinate such savagery: uproot such wildness (wild plants)

mead:	grassland
erst:	formerly

cowslip, burnet ... clover: all meadow-flowers

teems:	produces

docks ... thistles, kecksies, burs: wild plants which are useless or harmful

sciences:	knowledge, arts
diffused:	disordered
let:	obstacle

you would the peace: you wish to have peace

accept and peremptory answer: agreed and definitive reply

consign:	agree

articles ... stood on: items in the treaty are insisted on too strictly

the better Englishwoman: she distrusts flattering language, and so has a good quality of the English

mince it:	behave with affected refinement
measure:	(*a*) metre, (*b*) rhythmical movement, (*c*) degree, quantity
lay on:	deal blows
sit (line 141):	sit on horseback
jackanapes:	monkey
look greenly:	look lovesick

not worth sunburning: so sunburnt that it could be no worse

but for thy love ... no: Henry is mocking the poetic convention whereby lovers say that they will die if their love is unrequited. He has no intention of doing so

uncoined:	like metal that has not been minted. She is to avoid men who circulate from one lady to another, like money
his (line 163):	its

Saint Denis be my speed: may St Denis help me. He was the patron saint of France

truly-falsely:	truly in substance, but falsely in grammar

scambling:	fighting
Constantinople ... Turk:	The recovery of Constantinople (Byzantium) from the Turks was an ambition of Christian Europe; but the Turks did not capture Constantinople until 1453, after Henry's death
flower-de-luce:	the heraldic lily on the coat-of-arms of the French monarchy
know (line 210):	with a pun on the meaning 'have sexual intercourse'
moiety:	half, share
untempering:	unpersuasive
layer-up:	preserver, storer. Age causes wrinkles in the face, like those in a badly-stored garment
Plantagenet:	the surname of the English royal family from 1154 to 1485
broken music:	instrumental music in parts
nice:	unimportant
curtsy:	give way
list:	barrier
follows our places:	results from our high positions
condition:	disposition, temperament
circle:	the magic circle which a conjurer drew when he raised spirits. Here with a sexual pun
naked and blind:	Cupid, the god of love, was depicted as a blind naked boy
summered:	maintained
Bartholomew-tide:	St Bartholomew's day, 24 August. At this time of year, flies are sluggish and easily caught
moral:	parable, comparison
perspectively:	as if in a perspective (a picture constructed so as to give different pictures from different viewpoints)
look pale:	a reference to the white chalk cliffs near Dover and near Calais, where England and France are nearest
paction:	agreement
incorporate league:	alliance which makes them into one body (as in Christian marriage man and wife are said to become one flesh)
Sennet:	ceremonial fanfare on a trumpet

Epilogue

Henry lived only a short time, but lived greatly. He left England and France to his infant son: but so many people had a hand in his government that they lost France and caused England to bleed—events which have often been shown in our theatre.

NOTES AND GLOSSARY:

Mangling by starts: spoiling by giving only short portions
Small time: Henry died at the age of thirty-five
the world's best garden: France (see V.2.36)
his son: Henry VI (1421-71) was less than a year old when his father died. His reign saw the loss of France and civil war in England
our stage hath shown: in Shakespeare's three *Henry VI* plays
let this acceptance take: let this play (*Henry V*) be accepted

Part 3

Commentary

Date and sources

The play is dated fairly closely by a reference to the Earl of Essex, 'the General of our gracious Empress' in Ireland (see note on V. Chor. 30, p.43). This passage must have been written after March 1599, when Essex went to Ireland as Governor-General, and before September 1599, when he returned to England in disgrace, having bungled his mission completely.

The main sources for the play are two sixteenth-century history-books, one by Edward Hall (1548), the other by Raphael Holinshed (1577). There were probably a number of minor sources, including an anonymous play called *The Famous Victories of Henry V* (which included a scene showing Henry wooing Katherine); but Hall and Holinshed provided the bulk of the material.

Shakespeare shaped this historical material to make it into a play. There were too many events in Hall and Holinshed, and Shakespeare selected and compressed a good deal. For example, five years passed between the Battle of Agincourt and the final signing of the peace-treaty, and in that time there were further English invasions of France, but Shakespeare makes it seem as though the treaty followed quite soon after the battle. Again, the events depicted in the final scene of the play, when the peace is negotiated, in reality took place over a period of a year in 1519–20, and the meeting of the kings was merely for the formal ratification of what had been hammered out in long negotiations. Besides simplifying events in this way, Shakespeare sometimes selected or changed his material to make it express the themes of his play—the glorification of the English monarchy, the idealisation of Henry as the great warrior-king, the exaltation of the English at the expense of the French, the playing on patriotic feeling.

Medieval and Tudor kings

The plays in Shakespeare's history-cycle deal with late-medieval England, but they are also about Tudor England, Shakespeare's own time. The cycle depicts the breakdown of medieval English society, and ends with the coming of a new era, that of the Tudor monarchs, who restore peace and prosperity; and this is in accordance with official Tudor views of the history of the period. At the same time, there are resemblances

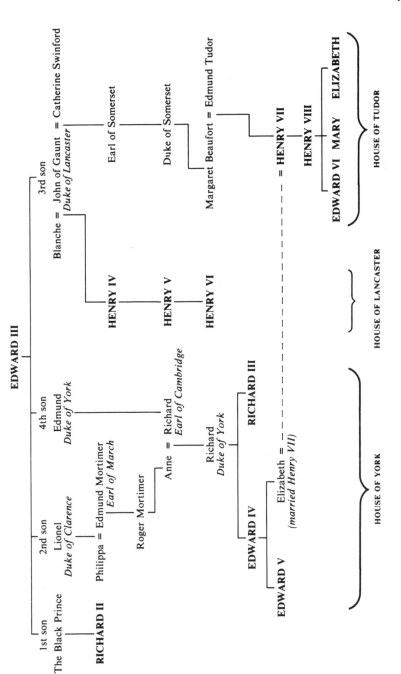

A SKELETON FAMILY TREE, SHOWING THE HOUSES OF YORK, LANCASTER AND TUDOR

For greater clarity, the fourth son of Edward III is shown before his third son

between the Lancastrian kings in the plays, Henry IV and Henry V, and the Tudors. The Lancastrians and the Tudors both came to the throne by successful rebellions, those of Henry IV and Henry VII; and the Tudor claim to the throne, such as it was, went back to the Lancastrian line. (See the skeleton family-tree, p.49.) Moreover, like the Tudors, Shakespeare's Lancastrians are modern men: in *Richard II*, Henry Bolingbroke is the practical, politic man; his businesslike efficiency replaces the medieval ceremoniousness, formality, and chivalry of the court of Richard II; for Bolingbroke becomes Henry IV: and, like the Tudors, he begins a new era.

In the other plays of the cycle, the political parallels between Lancastrians and Tudors are not made obvious: it would have been dangerous to draw comparisons between the usurper Henry IV and the founder of the Tudor dynasty Henry VII. But in *Henry V* the comparison can be allowed to become more open, because Henry is a figure who can, without danger, represent the aspirations of the Tudor monarchy: a strong king, bringing stability and order; a warrior king, who can rouse national feeling. The clearest way in which the parallel is suggested is in the insistence on Henry V's Welsh connection. The Tudors cultivated their Welsh ancestry as part of their mystique, and Henry VII named his eldest son Arthur (after the legendary Celtic king). In the play, similarly, a good deal is made of the fact that Henry was born in Wales: he himself refers twice to the fact (IV.1.51, IV.7.103), and Fluellen enlarges on the subject in his comparison of Henry with Alexander (IV.7.11–51) and again later in the scene (IV.7.104–12).

We can therefore see the play not only as a celebration of the warrior-king Henry V and the English who fought at Agincourt, but also as a celebration of the Tudor monarchs of the sixteenth century, of the national aspirations and feelings of the English in Shakespeare's time, and of the euphoria and sense of national unity in England in the years following the defeat of the Armada.

Patriotic feeling

One of the things the play does, then, is to arouse and focus feelings of patriotism. National feeling is linked to war, and the patriotism is military. This patriotic-military feeling is often evoked by the rhetoric of the play, like that of Henry's speech before Harfleur (III.1), beginning

> *Once more unto the breach, dear friends, once more,*
> *Or close the wall up with our English dead!*

The speech is an incitement to action, an assertion of the qualities of the 'noblest English', a reminder of past military achievements, a call to the army to be worthy of their ancestors and their country. The

Chorus, similarly, uses high rhetoric to arouse national feeling, as in the opening part of the Chorus to Act II, which is not merely a description of military preparations, but a glorification of the war. Even the French are made to contribute to the glorification of English military qualities, as when the French king reminds his court of the Battle of Crecy, where Henry's ancestors had defeated the French (II.4.50–62). This looking back to past military exploits is common in the play, and Crecy is mentioned elsewhere (e.g. I.2.102–14).

The French are consistently presented in a bad light in comparison to the English. The speed with which the English carry out their invasion is contrasted with the inefficiency of the French in meeting it (II.4, III.5). The French nobility are boastful and frivolous (III.7), whereas the English nobility are serious and resolute (IV.3). The Dauphin in particular is boastful, affected, and cowardly, in clear contrast to Henry.

The Scots, too, are referred to slightingly. Discussing the need to guard against a Scots invasion, Ely says

> *For once the eagle England being in prey,*
> *To her unguarded nest the weasel Scot*
> *Comes sneaking, and so sucks her princely eggs.*
> (I.2.169–71)

The national bias appears in the imagery: if the English attack France, they are like the eagle, the king of birds; but if the Scots attack England, they are like a cowardly weasel stealing the eagle's eggs. In the same scene, Canterbury refers contemptuously to the way in which, in Edward III's reign, the king of Scotland had been 'impounded as a stray' (I.2.160).

Moreover, episodes discreditable to the English are often omitted or changed. In III.3, Henry calls on the citizens of Harfleur to surrender; if they do not, he will sack the city; but if they surrender at once, they will escape this fate. The Governor of Harfleur responds to this by surrendering, and Henry orders Exeter to occupy the town and to 'Use mercy to them all' (III.3.54). But in reality the English *did* sack Harfleur, after it had surrendered—a subject on which Shakespeare is discreetly silent.

The manipulating of events for the glory of England is seen in the treatment of the battle. Shakespeare gives the total English dead as 29, and the French dead as 10,000 (IV.8.79–105). These are the most extreme figures he found anywhere in his sources. The very low figure for the English dead comes from Holinshed, but is merely mentioned by him, and is not his own estimate: he gives 500–600 as a more likely figure. Shakespeare makes the victory seem miraculous, not only by taking extreme figures for the losses, but also by saying nothing about the reasons for the extraordinary outcome of the battle. He simply shows a small English army being attacked by a vastly superior French force 'in plain shock and even play of battle' (IV.8.108), and the French army being massacred. Henry himself says that it is a miracle, and that all the credit must be given to God (IV.8.105–11). All the same, the audience no doubt assumed that God was fighting for the better side: it is constantly suggested in the play that the English are far better fighters than the French, and even Henry permits himself the boast that an Englishman is a match for three Frenchmen (III.6.147–48).

Such is Shakespeare's battle. In the real battle, Henry drew up his army across an opening between two woods, to avoid being outflanked by the French cavalry. Moreover, he chose the narrowest part of the opening so that, as the French advanced, their forces became progressively more squeezed together. The English drove pointed stakes into the ground in front of their lines, to protect them from cavalry, and from behind these stakes the English archers (famous for their accuracy) let fly a storm of arrows at the advancing French. The French cavalry attacked down the wings, but were driven back by arrows. The French infantry and dismounted cavalry advanced across flat muddy fields, which had been made even more boggy by heavy rain. The heavily-armed French had difficulty in moving across the muddy ground, and many of them were picked off by the English archers. Eventually they became completely bogged down, many of them having sunk in mud up to the thighs, and they never reached the English lines. When the English ran out of arrows, they advanced on foot, and, being relatively lightly armed, were able to move over the muddy ground and slaughter the immobilised French.

Shakespeare cannot have known *all* of this, but he certainly knew some of it: for example, the order to the English archers to drive in stakes is found in Holinshed; but Shakespeare does not mention it. It is clear that Shakespeare makes no attempt to give a plausible military reason for the astonishing result of the battle. He instead leaves the audience with the impression that the English are great fighters, and Henry a great leader of men. God fought on the English side, but this does not cancel out the credit to be given to the English for the way they fought. In any case, Henry's giving of the credit to God is a mark of his own piety and lack of boastfulness.

A play of outer action

Henry V is concerned with events rather than with character. We do not see men divided within themselves, torn between different desires or feelings, struggling with their consciences, as we do in many Shakespeare plays. Henry is a relatively simple character, brave and pious, knowing what is right and doing it without hesitation; he is never troubled by doubts or conflicting impulses. This absence of inner drama is reflected in the relative absence of soliloquy from the play. In the great tragedies, characters such as Macbeth and Hamlet have long soliloquies in which they reveal internal struggle; but such speeches are absent from *Henry V*. There are a few soliloquies, but they do not reflect inner struggle: for example, after his argument with the soldiers, Henry has a long soliloquy on ceremony (IV.1.222–77), but this contains no self-doubt or self-reproach: Henry knows that he is right, and comments bitterly on the hard lot of a king.

Because it is a play of outer events, some critics have argued that it is epic rather than dramatic. Epics are long narrative poems, the models being Homer's *Iliad* and Virgil's *Æneid*, the most famous long poems of ancient Greece and Rome respectively. Both handle heroic events connected with national history: the *Iliad* is about part of the siege of Troy by the Greeks, while the *Æneid* deals with the founding of the Roman state by the Trojan hero Æneas. According to Renaissance theory, the aim of an epic is to arouse admiration, and to inspire men to heroic deeds. *Henry V* clearly shares many of these characteristics, and its epic quality is increased by the use of a Chorus (which is very rare in Shakespeare plays). The narrative function of the Chorus increases the emphasis on events rather than on inner drama, and it also uses a high epic style, a dignified rhetoric calculated to inspire men to heroic actions.

Despite the concentration on outer action, the play lacks plot. We are simply given a sequence of historical events—deliberations on war, preparations for war, prosecution of the war, victory, peace-treaty. Into this historical sequence are threaded comic episodes of various kinds—the quarrel between Nym and Pistol, Princess Katherine learning English, Pistol eating the leek, and so on. So the play is episodic, that is, it consists of a series of episodes which do not follow inevitably from some initial situation, but are to some extent arbitrary. The unity of the play is of a different kind, given by its overall purpose, and often achieved by contrasts: for example, the scenes depicting the French nobility before Agincourt are clearly contrasted with the scenes depicting Henry and the English nobility. But above all, unity is given to the play by its central character, and the way in which nearly all episodes contribute to the picture of the ideal warrior-king.

The ideal Christian king

Henry V is a one-man play, dominated by its central character. Henry speaks about one-third of the words in the play, and no other character can compete with him in interest.

J.H. Walter has argued that Shakespeare's presentation of Henry was influenced by works on the ideal ruler*. There was a tradition of such works from classical antiquity onwards, and there were some well-known ones in the sixteenth century. Walter points out close parallels between the character of Henry and the ideals laid down in such works.

The ideal ruler, according to these works, is a Christian, supports the church, and is versed in theology. He is learned. He is just, yet merciful, and he does not take personal revenge. He exercises self-control. He takes the advice of wise counsellors. He is familiar with the ordinary people, but is not corrupted by his contact with them. He is deeply concerned with the preservation of his country, and is burdened with affairs of state which keep him awake at night. His kingdom is like the human body, where the parts work harmoniously together; idlers and parasites are banished or executed. He does not lightly embark on war, which causes the deaths of innocent people. He avoids flattery. And it is desirable for him to be married.

Henry's Christian piety is stressed throughout the play. Ely says that he is 'a true lover of the holy Church' (I.1.23), and Canterbury praises his learning in theology (I.1.38–40). Such piety and learning seem surprising in a king who had been wild in his youth, and Canterbury attributes the change in Henry to a religious conversion that took place when his father died (I.1.25–31). He also praises Henry for his learning in other fields—commonwealth affairs, war, politics—and his eloquence (I.1.38–52).

Henry's justice is seen in his condemnation of Scroop, Cambridge, and Grey: he seeks no personal revenge on them, but the safety of the state requires their deaths (II.2.174–77). His clemency is seen in the pardoning of the man who had spoken against him (II.2.39–60). His self-control is illustrated in the scene where he receives the gift of tennis-balls from the Dauphin: he is clearly angry, but it is a controlled anger which makes his threats of retribution all the more terrifying. His listening to wise counsellors is shown in the debate on the proposed war—first on its justice (I.2.1–100), then on its practicability (I.2.100–221). Henry himself plays an important part in the debate, for example in raising the problem of the Scots (I.2.136–39), but most of the time he listens to the views of others—Canterbury, Ely, Exeter, Westmorland—and, having heard them out, he makes a firm decision (I.2.223–34).

We see Henry mixing with ordinary people when, the night before Agincourt, he goes around the camp in disguise (IV.1.35–222). In the soliloquy that follows (IV.1.223–77), we hear of the burdens that Henry carries as a king, and the hours of sleeplessness he spends labouring in the interests of the commonwealth.

The harmonious orderliness of Henry's kingdom is suggested by

*Shakespeare, *King Henry V*, ed J.H. Walter, Methuen, London, 1954, pp.xvi–xviii.

Canterbury's comparison with a hive of bees (I.2.187–204). And just as, in the hive, the idle drones are put to death, so in Henry's kingdom the idlers and parasites are punished: Falstaff is dismissed from the King's company (in *Henry IV Part 2*), and Bardolph and Nym are hanged (IV.4.68–71).

Henry starts a war, but not until he is convinced of its justice (I.2.8–100). He knows of the horrors of war, as we see in his threats to Harfleur (III.3.1–43); but he has also thought seriously about his responsibilities in the matter, as we see in his argument with the soldiers (IV.1.120–80).

Henry the man

Henry, however, is not just a character out of a handbook: Shakespeare also gives him many qualities of his own. We have already seen his single-mindedness and freedom from self-doubt. He has great serenity and cheerfulness in difficulties, which helps to maintain the morale of his followers. He has a sense of humour, and is not above playing a practical joke on Fluellen (IV.7.149–63). He is a plain practical man, with little time for shows and ceremonies, and able to converse on easy terms with people of any rank. This blunt practicality is carried to extremes in the scene where he woos Katherine (V.2). Nevertheless, he has great eloquence, especially when he is inciting men to action, as at Harfleur (III.1), but also elsewhere, as when he laments the treachery of Scroop, which seems like 'Another fall of man' (II.2.142).

Many critics have emphasised the limitations of his character. He is, it has been said, a man of action, and has the narrowness of the man of action: he has a limited practical intellect; he lacks imagination; he has a commonplace mind; he is cold, and never at any time expresses affection for anybody. This last accusation is not literally true: Henry expresses grief at the death of York and Suffolk (IV.6.32–34); but he does so very briefly, and immediately turns back to the practical business of the battle. And he tells Katherine that he loves her (V.2.219); but he makes it clear that he is fully in command of his feelings:

> If thou canst love me for this, take me; if not, to say to thee that I shall die is true—but for thy love, by the Lord, no.
>
> (V.2.149–51)

This is not the language of an impassioned lover.

Some critics have gone further, and made serious attacks on Henry's integrity: he is a hypocrite, who commits unjustified aggression under the guise of piety: his attack on France is aimed at diverting attention from the weakness of his own claim to the English throne; he knows that his claim to France is a weak one, and encourages Canterbury to give him a plausible pretext; he is ruthless and cold-blooded, and at Agincourt orders his prisoners to be killed without a qualm or a moment's hesitation. This view of Henry's character would clearly undermine the interpretation of the play that has been presented so far.

Is the play ironic?

If we take the play at face-value, it is a patriotic work; but if Henry's character is interpreted unsympathetically, a very different view can be taken; and some critics have argued that, far from being a glorification of nationalism and military achievement, the play is, on the contrary, an attack on them. Gerald Gould, for example, says that Shakespeare presents Henry as a brutal and degrading militarist;* the play is a satire on monarchical government, on imperialism, and on war; Henry is a hypocrite, and never performs any act except for political advantage; he is cold-blooded and ruthless; he knows that his claim to the French throne is unjustified; his aggression against France had been planned before Canterbury's explanation of his claim; and Bardolph and Nym are hanged for doing on a small scale what Henry himself has done on a large one.

It is easy for a present-day reader to see Henry as an aggressor and a militarist, but it is unlikely that Shakespeare's contemporaries would have taken this view, and the evidence of the play is against it. If Henry were a hypocritical schemer, this fact would emerge clearly from the play (for example, in ironical comment and in soliloquy); but it does not. Gould suggests that Henry is hypocritical even in his soliloquies; but this disregards the normal Elizabethan convention whereby, in soliloquies, characters reveal their true selves. If a character is a villain, he tells the audience so.

As regards the claim to the French throne, in sixteenth-century England it was generally believed that this claim was a just one. If Shakespeare intended his audience to see the claim as fraudulent, there would have been some indication of this. But nobody in the play answers Canterbury's long justification of the English claim in I.2. There are scenes at the French court, like II.4, where it would have been perfectly possible for a spokesman for the French to dispute the English claim; but this is never done. Even if the English claim were just, the true heir to the French throne would, admittedly, not have been Henry, but Edmund Mortimer, Earl of March; but this fact is not mentioned in the play either. Had Shakespeare wished, the claims of Mortimer could easily have been stated, as they are in other plays in the history-cycle; but *Henry V* is silent on the point. Nor is there any mention in the play

*G. Gould, 'Irony and Satire in Henry V', in *Shakespeare, Henry V: A casebook*, ed. M. Quinn, Macmillan, London, 1969, pp.81–94.

of a cunning political motive for the war with France: on the contrary, Henry is shown as being most scrupulous about the justice of his cause.

Moreover, the changes that Shakespeare makes in his source-material are ones that glorify Henry and the English. As we have seen, there is no mention of the sacking of Harfleur by the English, and the account of Agincourt is very flattering to them. If Shakespeare was satirising English militarism, this was a strange way to do it.

Finally, the use of the Chorus is difficult to reconcile with Gould's view, according to which we should have to interpret what the Chorus says as ironical, or at least as not representing Shakespeare's own views. But this is contrary to the normal practice of the Elizabethan theatre, in which a figure like the Chorus is taken to be not just another character in the play but a truthful spokesman for the author.

Extreme views like Gould's, therefore, are implausible. It could nevertheless be argued that there are passages which invite the audience to be critical about the war or about Henry, and that the play is therefore not a simple glorification of nationalism.

A critical light on the war

The first scene of the play shows clearly that Canterbury and Ely have ulterior motives for encouraging Henry to go to war. So the audience is bound to suspect the Archbishop's sincerity when, in the following scene, he argues the justice of Henry's claim to France. Nevertheless, the fact remains that nobody in the play contradicts his arguments.

Again, there are passages in the play that evoke the unpleasant aspects of war. There is Henry's threat to the citizens of Harfleur (III.3.1–43), in which he paints a picture of the English soldiers raping women, dashing old men's heads against walls, spitting infants on pikes. The night before Agincourt, Williams similarly evokes the carnage of battle:

> But if the cause be not good, the King himself hath a heavy reckoning to make, when all those legs, and arms, and heads, chopped off in a battle, shall join together at the latter day ... some swearing, some crying for a surgeon, some upon their wives left poor behind them, some upon the debts they owe, some upon their children rawly left.
> (IV.1.130–36)

We also see how war attracts the scum of society. Nym, Bardolph, and Pistol go to the war for loot:

> *Let us to France, like horse-leeches, my boys,*
> *To suck, to suck, the very blood to suck!*
> (II.3.52–53)

There is also one long speech which deplores war and its effects, and praises peace, spoken by Burgundy in the final scene of the play (V.2.23–67). He calls peace the 'dear nurse of arts, plenties, and joyful births' (V.2.35). He draws a vivid picture of the results of war in France: the countryside going to ruin, crops rotting, children growing up like savages, learning and the arts decaying. This is indeed most eloquent; but it is noteworthy that it is not said until the English have won the war. Once English military and political objectives have been achieved, the audience can be allowed the luxury of a speech in praise of peace.

There is also one place in the play (IV.1.125–84) where the King's responsibility for the war is discussed. The soldiers Bates and Williams argue that they have no responsibility for deciding whether they are fighting in a just cause: they are bound to obey the King, and if his cause is unjust the King himself will answer for it at the Day of Judgement. In reply, Henry argues that the King has no responsibility for the sins of his soldiers: if a soldier is a murderer or a robber, he has to answer to God for that himself. The soldiers end up by agreeing with him; but it is a striking fact that Henry says nothing about the justice of his cause, which was the starting-point of the discussion. Has he deliberately evaded the question? Or does he simply take it for granted that his cause is just, and that this is a matter of state which should not be discussed by common soldiers?

There are, then, passages in the play that turn a critical light on the war, and perhaps even question its justice. But they are very few compared with the speeches and incidents that glorify war and the English, and it could therefore be argued that the overall effect of the play is to arouse rather simple and unqualified patriotic and military feelings.

The absence of politics

Henry V avoids the discussion of sensitive political issues. If Henry was to be the ideal king, and if the play was also to be seen as a glorification of the Tudor monarchs of the sixteenth century, then obviously the play could not discuss awkward topics like the weakness of Henry's title to the English crown. So Shakespeare suppresses facts of which he was well aware (as can be seen from the other plays), and tends to sweep politics under the carpet.

We have already seen one example: the fact that there is no mention of any ulterior motive for the war with France. At the end of *Henry IV Part 2*, the dying Henry IV talks to his son about the devious ways by which he had obtained the crown, and advises him to 'busy giddy minds With foreign quarrels', to divert attention from domestic politics. In reply, Prince Hal asserts his determination to hold by force the crown which his father had 'won'; and in the last scene of the play, when he has just become king, we hear that he is already contemplating an attack on France. But in *Henry V* no mention is made of the motive urged by Henry IV: the King is shown as being scrupulously concerned with the justice of his claim and with nothing else.

Another case is the treatment of the conspiracy of Cambridge, Scroop, and Grey. The Chorus to Act II says repeatedly that the motive for their plot was money: *treacherous crowns* (22), *for the gilt of France* (26), *the sum is paid* (33). Exeter says the same at the beginning of II.2: *for a foreign purse* (10). And so does Henry when the conspirators are unmasked later in the same scene: *for a few light crowns* (89), *foreign hire* (100), *the golden earnest* (169), *you would have sold your King* (170). Cambridge, indeed, does hint at a different motive:

> *For me, the gold of France did not seduce,*
> *Although I did admit it as a motive*
> *The sooner to effect what I intended.* (II.2.155–57)

But he says no more, and the audience is left in the dark. Shakespeare, however, knew perfectly well what other motive Cambridge had for the conspiracy: it was to put Edmund Mortimer on the throne, on the grounds that the Mortimers had a better title to the throne than the Lancastrians. Shakespeare had explained this in detail in *Henry VI Part 1*, and it was also mentioned in his source-material for *Henry V*. But this brings up the whole question of the Lancastrian usurpation, and so cannot appear in a play which equates Lancastrians with Tudors. In Henry's long reproach to the conspirators (II.2.79–144), the whole emphasis is personal, not political. He is pained and astonished that a personal friend like Scroop, who had seemed a model nobleman, should have plotted his death. The speech is very eloquent and touching, but is completely silent on the whole political background.

Throughout *Henry V* the Lancastrian usurpation is hushed up; this is in strong contrast to the *Henry IV* plays, where the subject is discussed at great length. The Epilogue to *Henry V* does refer to the civil wars that broke out in England after Henry's death, but it attributes these, not to the Lancastrian usurpation, but to the fact that too many people had a hand in running the kingdom. In only one place in *Henry V* is the usurpation mentioned—Henry's prayer before Agincourt:

> *Not today, O Lord,*
> *O not today, think not upon the fault*
> *My father made in compassing the crown!*
> *I Richard's body have interred new,*
> *And on it have bestowed more contrite tears*
> *Than from it issued forced drops of blood.* (IV.1.285–90)

Here Henry admits his father's 'fault' in seizing the crown, and asks for it to be pardoned. But it does not occur to him to wonder whether one can ask God for pardon when one has no intention of giving up the proceeds of the crime. Henry, indeed, was not himself the murderer and usurper; but he is profiting from those crimes, to which his family owes the crown. The moral question involved is one that Shakespeare raised in other plays, but not here; for to raise it is to risk undermining the play. *Henry V* is the one Shakespeare history play that sets out to give an uncritical glorification of the Tudor monarchy and its ideals. To do this, he omits historical facts of which he was fully aware, and suspends his own powers of moral and political analysis.

The absence of Falstaff

In the *Henry IV* plays, one of the most popular characters had been Sir John Falstaff, the fat scoundrel knight who was one of Prince Hal's tavern-companions. In the Epilogue to *Henry IV Part 2*, Shakespeare had told his audience that he was going to continue the story (in *Henry V*), and that Falstaff would be in this continuation. But Falstaff does not appear in *Henry V*; and in II.3 we have the Hostess's account of his death—an account both comic and moving.

Some critics believe that originally Falstaff did appear in the play, but that Shakespeare revised it and removed him, transferring some of his part to Pistol. The theory is based on certain inconsistencies in the play (for example, the fact that the Chorus to Act II suggests that the scene is about to move to Southampton, which it does not), and on the occurrence of the name *Doll* instead of *Nell* at V.1.77 (see note in Part 2 above).

The revision theory is plausible, but not proved. What is certain is that Shakespeare promised that Falstaff should appear in *Henry V*, but later changed his mind. Various reasons have been suggested for this: that the actor who played Falstaff was no longer available; that there was pressure on the actors from an influential family, who thought that Falstaff was a reflection on them; that Shakespeare feared that Falstaff would steal the limelight from Henry.

We do not know which of these theories, if any, is right. But certainly *Henry V* loses a great deal, compared with the *Henry IV* plays, from the absence of Falstaff; for Falstaff is one of the great comic characters of literature. But *Henry V* loses, not just comedy, but also the voice of a critical commentator. In *Henry IV*, Falstaff is unscrupulous, cynical, self-centred; but he is also highly intelligent, and makes penetrating comments on people and events. *Henry V* lacks any such critical voice—a voice that questions people's motives, ridicules their ideals, pricks the bubble of their pretensions. For example, in *Henry IV Part*

I there is a famous speech by Falstaff on honour (military glory), which he dismisses as useless and dangerous. In *Henry V*, the King is represented as a great seeker after honour, as when he refuses to share Westmorland's wish for more men at Agincourt (IV.3.18–33); and there is no Falstaff to comment on this. So one result of the death of Falstaff is that the patriotic and military ideals of the play are nowhere ridiculed or criticised; and this makes it easier for the play to be a simple idealisation of the warrior-king and the noble warlike English.

Some commentators suggest that the critical role of Falstaff is taken over in *Henry V* by Bardolph, Nym, and Pistol. But those characters have neither the wit nor the intelligence of Falstaff, and are incapable of making penetrating comments. Nor is there anything in the play which makes us compare their behaviour as thieves with Henry's behaviour in invading France (as Gould suggests). In *Henry IV* we are obviously meant to see parallels of this kind: for example, in *Henry IV Part I* there is a tavern-scene where Prince Hal and Falstaff do some amateur acting, parodying a scene which is going to take place the following day when the prince visits his father. There is nothing resembling this in *Henry V*.

The other characters

Henry's character is the only one developed in any detail; most of the others are very slightly sketched. The English noblemen are simply model soldiers and counsellors, and are not distinguished from one another: if some of Westmorland's speeches were given to Exeter or Bedford, nobody would notice any difference. Canterbury and Ely are depicted as slightly unscrupulous politicians, but are not studied in depth. The French noblemen at Agincourt are boastful and over-confident: the Dauphin is more foolish than the others, Orleans more flattering, the Constable more sensible; but that is about as far as the characterisation goes. There are two groups of characters worth considering at slightly greater length: the four captains, and the three scoundrels.

Bardolph, Nym, and Pistol

These three cowards, cheats, and thieves provide an element of low-life comedy. Much of it comes from the contrast between their brave words and their cowardly actions, as when Nym and Pistol quarrel but are afraid to fight (II.1). Each of them is given a few obvious comic characteristics. Bardolph has a simple physical one: he has a very red face and nose, about which people make jokes. Even when Fluellen relates that Bardolph is to be hanged for robbing a church, the account ends with a joke at his expense—'but his nose is executed, and his fire's out' (III.6.102–3). Nym acts the part of the strong silent man. When he does speak, he is fond of a few modish expressions like *that's the humour of it* and *in fair terms*, which he misuses or uses in a very vague sense. J. Dover Wilson suggests that Nym also had a comic physical characteristic, namely long shaggy hair*: he is called *Iceland dog* (II.1.38) and *hound of Crete* (II.1.70).

The most cowardly and the most boastful is Pistol, and he suffers the biggest comic discomfiture of the play, when Fluellen makes him eat the leek (V.1). His speech is extremely comic. He always speaks in verse (whereas the other low-life characters use prose), and he uses a bombastic style imitated from popular plays of the period. The verse has constant alliteration, and simple monotonous rhythms, as in

> *Let floods o'erswell, and fiends for food howl on!*
> (II.1.89)

It is full of ridiculous pompous phrases: Pistol says *exhale* (II.1.59) when he means 'draw your sword'; and when he wants his wife to stop crying, he says 'clear thy crystals' (II.3.51). Because of his greater cowardice, he is the only one of the three to survive the campaign.

With these three can be mentioned the Boy, and Hostess Quickly. The Boy is precocious, witty, and perceptive, and he gives devastating accounts of the three men (III.2.28–53, IV.4.66–72). Hostess Quickly is good-natured and foolish, and uses strings of long words which she misunderstands.

The Four Captains

The inclusion of the four captains—English, Welsh, Irish, and Scots—suggests that the English crown has claims over the whole of the British Isles. Wales had indeed been subject to the English crown since about 1300. Ireland had been invaded by the English in the twelfth century, since when the Kings of England had claimed to rule it, though they seldom had effective power except in the east of the country, and were faced with frequent rebellions. The medieval English kings had also claimed overlordship of Scotland, but had never been able to make their claim good. The union of the crowns of England and Scotland did not take place until 1603, when James VI of Scotland became James I of England. In including a sympathetic portrait of a Scots captain, Shakespeare may have been looking forward to that event. It is even possible that he did not put the Scots captain in until after 1603; for the scene in which he appears is not in the 'bad' quarto of 1600, and

*Shakespeare, *King Henry V*, Ed. J.D. Wilson, Cambridge University Press, London, 1947, p 135.

may be a later addition. In any case, the fact that a Welsh, Irish, and Scots captain are shown fighting side by side with the English under an English king is a clear indication of the aspirations of the English crown.

For most of the play there are only two captains, for the Scot and the Irishman appear in only one scene (III.2), and then briefly. The Irishman, Macmorris, is excitable and touchy. The Scot, Jamy, is grave and thoughtful. Both have distinctive regional forms of speech (see the notes on Act III, Scene 2 in Part 2 above).

Gower and Fluellen play a more substantial part. Gower is an example of a plain honest man, simple, sensible, and brave. Fluellen is a more remarkable character, and deserves a section to himself.

Fluellen

Fluellen is excitable, talkative, hot-tempered, pedantic, good-natured, brave, proud of being Welsh. An amusing example of his talkativeness is seen the night before Agincourt (IV.1), when he tells Gower to make less noise, and explains the military importance of quietness; and all this while Gower says only sixteen words, while Fluellen utters over a hundred. His excitability and quick temper are seen when Williams challenges the glove in his cap (IV.8); and the episode also shows his good nature, for when he learns the truth he offers Williams money and praises his courage (though he cannot resist giving him a little sermon on keeping out of quarrels). His national pride is apparent when he beats Pistol and makes him eat the leek (V.1.15–64).

Fluellen's pedantry is seen in his constant reference to ancient authors. He is trained in the new humanist learning, and believes that all wisdom is to be found in the writings of ancient Greece and Rome. He is easily impressed by words, which explains why he is at first mistaken about Pistol, who (he says) had done 'gallant service' at the bridge (III.6.12–15). It turns out, however, that he had not seen Pistol *do* anything, but merely talk—'I'll assure you, 'a uttered as prave words at the pridge as you shall see in a summer's day' (III.6.62–63).

Fluellen's faith in the classics extends to warfare: everything that needs to be known about war can be learned from the ancients. He despises Macmorris, because the Irishman knows nothing about the 'true disciplines of the wars', which are 'the Roman disciplines' (III.2.68–71), and is eager to argue with him. The difference of opinion between Fluellen and Macmorris was a genuine matter of dispute in Shakespeare's time. There were military theorists who argued that classical authors were still the best guide to warfare; in opposition to them were soldiers who argued that such things as gunpowder had altered the techniques of war.

Above all it is Fluellen's eccentric speech which makes him such a striking comic character. His native language is Welsh, and for him English is a foreign language; he speaks it fluently and eloquently, but in a manner all his own. He has many peculiarities of pronunciation, like replacing 'b' by 'p', which lead to ridiculous expressions like *Alexander the Pig* (IV.7.12–13); here he first makes the mistake of saying *big* instead of *great*, and then by his mispronunciation turns the famous Alexander into an animal. His grammar and phraseology are also very odd: examples will be found in the notes in Part 2 above. At the same time, as a humanist trained in classical literature and rhetoric, he aims at eloquence by the use of figures, as when he says:

> Alexander, God knows and you know, in his rages, and his furies, and his wraths, and his cholers, and his moods, and his displeasures, and his indignations, and also being a little intoxicates in his prains, did in his ales and his angers, look you, kill his best friend Cleitus.
> (IV.7.32–37)

Here Fluellen is using the rhetorical technique of piling up words of the same meaning (*rages, furies, wraths, cholers, moods, displeasures, indignations*) but produces an odd effect by making all these words plural instead of singular, and then makes the grammatical mistake of *intoxicates* instead of *intoxicated*. The passage comes from Fluellen's comparison of Henry with Alexander, which contains the splendid observation that there is a river in Macedon, and there is a river in Monmouth, 'and there is salmons in both' (IV.7.29). The combination of pedantry, absurdity, eloquence, and eccentric English makes Fluellen an irresistibly comic character.

The Two Armies

There are striking differences between the French army and the English army. The French leaders squabble (III.7), whereas the English nobility are united (e.g. the opening of IV.3). We see an easy relationship between English soldiers of all ranks: the captains Fluellen and Gower converse easily with the King (IV.7. 90–112), and the ordinary soldier is on free-and-easy terms with the officer (Williams and Gower at the opening of IV.8). The ordinary soldiers are independent-minded, as we see in their discussion with the King (IV.1.90-222). When the King summons Williams to speak to him (IV.7.116), the soldier is unabashed in the King's presence. By contrast, we never see a French nobleman speak to an ordinary soldier. The French herald is shocked that peasants should be drenched in the blood of princes (IV.7.75–76); whereas Henry speaks eloquently in praise of the English yeomanry (III.1.25–30).

The impression that emerges is that the English army is truly national, uniting people of all classes in harmonious co-operation, whereas the French army is led by an isolated élite.

The language of the play

Henry V is partly in verse and partly in prose. Prose is normal in low-life and comic scenes. Scenes dealing with princes and noblemen are usually in verse, but may be in prose if the subject is not elevated: the French nobility use prose in III.7, when they are just chatting; Henry and Burgundy use prose when they are joking together (V.2.277–322); the King's wooing of Katherine is in prose, because he is being the plain blunt man who is incapable of art. Henry also speaks prose in his encounters with Pistol and the soldiers in IV.1; this is part of his disguise, but he speaks a more formal and artistic prose than the soldiers (for example IV.1.143–80).

Verse is used for the more serious and exalted parts of the play. Normally it is blank verse, that is, unrhymed iambic pentameter. An iambic pentameter has the following basic pattern:

Whŏ Pró-/lŏgue-like / yŏur húm-/blĕ pá-/tiĕnce práy.
(Prologue 33)

The line consists of five feet (metrical units) each consisting of an unstressed syllable followed by a stressed one. On this basic pattern the poet makes variations, and may depart quite a long way from it. Two common variations are the inversion of a foot, and the use of a foot with two unstressed syllables. Both are seen in the opening line of the play:

Ó fŏr / ă Múse / ŏf fíre / thăt wŏuld / ăscénd.

Here the first foot is inverted, and the fourth consists of two unstressed syllables.

Occasionally, rhyme is used, especially in the last two lines of a scene, giving a sense of finality. The Epilogue is rhymed, and is a sonnet, with the rhyme-scheme *'abab cdcd efef gg.'*

The style of the verse passages is dignified and formal, sometimes rising to ardour (as in III.1), and sometimes to a moving eloquence (as in IV.6.7–32). It is usually expansive rather than rapid, enlarging on a subject rather than hurrying onward; and it often uses those figures of rhetoric that involve repetition and accumulation. The expansiveness is seen in Henry's reproach to Scroop, which occupies nearly fifty lines (II.2.94–142). The following is part of it:

Show men dutiful?
Why, so didst thou. Seem they grave and learned?

Why, so didst thou. Come they of noble family?
Why, so didst thou. Seem they religious?
Why, so didst thou. Or are they spare in diet,
Free from gross passion or of mirth or anger,
Constant in spirit, not swerving with the blood,
Garnished and decked in modest complement,
Not working with the eye without the ear,
And but in purged judgement trusting neither?
Such and so finely bolted didst thou seem.

(II.2.127–37)

In the first five lines there is a figure of repetition, a series of questions all given the same answer; then follows a heaping-up of good qualities which Scroop had seemed to have. This leisurely cumulative style is typical of the play, and even in the heat of battle we can pause for a long description of the deaths of York and Suffolk (IV.6.7–32).

In most of Shakespeare's plays there are recurrent groups of words that affect the atmosphere of the play and often point to the themes it is handling. Spurgeon has pointed out that *Henry V* frequently evokes swift soaring movement, suggestive of the flight of birds: there are many references to wings, like *our wings* (I.2.308) and *winged thoughts* (V.Chor.8). These are often connected with the Chorus's appeal to the audience to use their imaginations, but also suggest the aspirations and the speed of Henry and the English army.

The warlike qualities of Henry and the English are suggested by references to wild animals, hunting dogs, and birds of prey: lions (I.2.109, I.2.124, IV.3.93), the eagle (I.2.169), hounds (Prol. 7, III.1.131), the tiger (III.1.6). The violence of war is suggested by references to storms, especially the stormy sea: the tide pouring into a breach (I.2.149), waters sucked into a whirlpool (II.4.10), the ocean cutting away the base of a cliff (III.1.12–14), tempest, thunder, and earthquake (II.4.99–100).

Effective use is made of proper names. The names of the English nobility are usually also English place-names, so that such names summon up the towns and countryside and atmosphere of England itself—'Bedford and Exeter, Warwick and Talbot, Salisbury and Gloucester' (IV.3.53–54). The words *England* and *English* occur very frequently. And the King's own simplicity and Englishness are suggested by the frequent use of the pet-name *Harry*. These uses of proper names reinforce the play's appeal to patriotic sentiment.

Part 4

Hints for study

General advice

You must know the play really well: read it time and time again. You should know it so well that, if you are asked a question about it, you can immediately think of events or characters that help you to answer it, and quote short passages from memory. When you write about the play, show that you know it well: support your argument by detailed reference to what happens in the play, and with short quotations. Read the play at different speeds: at first, you will sometimes want to work through it slowly, using the notes, to make sure that you understand everything; but remember that it is a play, so sometimes read it straight through without a break. And try to imagine it being acted as you read it, or even act it out yourself, reading aloud.

Secondly, you should *think* about the play. There are many different views about what the play means, how effective it is, how Shakespeare gains his effects, and so on. In the end, you yourself must decide what you think about these things. Obviously you want to know what other people have said about the play, and in Part 5 below there are some suggestions for further reading; but the final test for any view is to be found in the text of the play itself. So when you are thinking about the play, have the text open in front of you, and constantly check whether the view you are considering is borne out by what is said and done in the play. Do not make up your mind too quickly, or accept immediately the view of some critic; first weigh all the evidence you can find in the play. It is especially necessary not to shut your eyes to evidence which contradicts your own first view; on the contrary, you should look for such evidence, and see where it leads you. Indeed, unless you develop the habit of considering the evidence that contradicts your own view, you will not be *thinking* at all.

Thirdly, you must practise writing about the play. You need to be able to write simply and clearly, to arrange your material methodically, and to present evidence for your viewpoint. Sometimes, you should write an essay at leisure, with the text of the play open in front of you. But, if you are working for an examination, you should also practise writing essays under examination-conditions—in a limited time, and without the text of the play. Here are some suggestions for topics to study, followed by some essay-questions.

Topics for study

Does Henry's character develop in the course of the play? Examine in particular I.2, III.1, III.3, IV.1, IV.3, V.2. Does he decide things for himself more in the later scenes? Do any personal characteristics first emerge in the later scenes?

Analyse the characters of (a) Pistol, (b) Fluellen, (c) the Dauphin, (d) Gower, and (e) Williams. In each case, examine what the character says, what he does, and what other people say about him.

Why are there so few women in the play? Examine what is contributed to the play by the four that do appear.

Examine the following episodes in the play, and say what it is that makes each of them amusing: (a) The quarrel of Nym and Pistol (II.1); (b) The account of the death of Falstaff (II.3); (c) Katherine's English lesson (III.4); (d) The conversation of the French nobles before Agincourt (III.7); (e) Fluellen's comparison of Henry with Alexander (IV.7); (f) Pistol eating the leek (V.1); and (g) Henry's wooing of Katherine (V.2). In addition, try to decide what makes (b) moving as well.

Has *Henry V* got a plot? What scenes contribute nothing to the main action? What is the function of these scenes?

Examine the episode of the killing of the prisoners. Is the killing justified? What does it show us about Henry?

Examine the things said by the French (a) about Henry, and (b) about the English generally. Do their views change in the course of the play? What contribution do these utterances made to the play?

Examine all the speeches of the Chorus, and list the various uses Shakespeare makes of it. It is very rare for Shakespeare to use a Chorus; why does he use one so extensively in *Henry V*?

Look at the references made in the play to *dogs*. What are such references mainly used for? Look similarly at the references to (a) the sun, and (b) hell, devils, and demons.

Make a list of the various purposes for which prose is used in the play. Choose a short example to illustrate each use.

Analyse the following speeches: (a) Henry's reproach to Scroop (II.2.93-142); (b) Henry's speech at the breach at Harfleur (III.1); (c) 'This day is called the feast of Crispian' (IV.3.40-67); and (d) Burgundy's speech arguing for peace (V.2.23-67). With each speech, examine the course of its argument, any changes in mood or tone or attitude that take place in it, the kinds of effects it produces, and the methods used to produce them (for example particular metaphors or comparisons, rhetorical devices).

Collect all the evidence you can find in the play that suggests that we are meant to see (a) Henry, and (b) the war in a critical or unsympathetic light. Weigh this against contrary evidence.

Essay questions

If you have worked at the play in the ways suggested above, you should be able to tackle the following essay questions. They are arranged roughly in order of difficulty, and more elementary students are advised not to attempt the later ones at first.

(1) What are the functions of the Chorus in *Henry V*?

(2) What do we learn about Henry (*a*) from his wooing of Katherine, (*b*) from his dealings with Williams and Bates, and (*c*) from his handling of the conspiracy of Cambridge, Scroop, and Grey?

(3) Give an account of the character of Fluellen, and discuss his contribution to the effect of the play.

(4) Explain what is meant by the statement that *Henry V* is episodic. Do you agree that it is? What kind of unity do you think the play has?

(5) What is meant by the statement that *Henry V* has epic qualities? What methods does Shakespeare use to achieve these qualities?

(6) Do you agree that Act V of *Henry V* is inferior to the rest of the play, and comes as an anticlimax?

(7) Give an account of the different kinds of comedy that are to be found in *Henry V*. What do these various comic elements contribute to the play?

(8) 'Not until towards the end of Act III, as we read the play, does the humanity of the king begin to engage our hearts' (J. Dover Wilson). What are the 'human' qualities of Henry, and in what episodes of the play are they especially revealed?

(9) 'It is one of the curiosities of literature that *Henry V* should have been seen so often as a simple glorification of the hero-king ... On the evidence of the play itself, Shakespeare's attitude towards the King is complex and critical' (L.C. Knights). Examine the evidence in the play for a 'complex and critical' attitude towards Henry.

(10) 'Behind the action [of a play] ... there must be some spiritually significant idea, or it will hang lifeless. And this is what is lacking in *Henry V*' (H. Granville-Barker). Discuss this view of *Henry V*.

Writing an essay

When you write an essay, write about the subject set, and about nothing else. If you are asked a question on the character of Henry, do not discuss the life of Shakespeare, or sixteenth-century politics, or the Elizabethan stage: if you do, your examiner will just cross such passages out, and you will have wasted time and effort. Do not even take it for granted that your essay has to have some kind of introductory paragraph. Students are often taught that an essay must begin with an introduction and end with a conclusion; but this is not necessarily the case, and the introductions that students write are often mere padding. If you are asked to write an essay on the subject 'Does the character of Henry change between Act I and Act III of the play?', the best way to begin your essay is with some such words as 'In Act I of the play Henry is . . .'; this gets you straight into the subject without fuss or waste of time.

Secondly, your essay must be planned. Do not start writing without thinking, but jot down ideas; then arrange these under headings, which will provide the sections of your essay; and note down suitable examples under each heading. When you have the plan of the essay clear, begin writing. Try to write in a plain straightforward way, but nevertheless with enthusiasm: an essay usually reads better if we feel that the writer is enjoying what he is talking about.

Specimen essay-plan

As an example of a simple plan for an essay, let us take the first essay-subject from our list, 'What are the functions of the Chorus in *Henry V*?'. After jotting down ideas, you might arrive at a plan like the following: (*i*) Simple narrative; (*ii*) Arousing expectation; (*iii*) Interpretation; (*iv*) Imaginative recreation; (*v*) Epic quality.

Under these headings can be grouped the various ideas and examples that have been thought of, and we get a fuller plan, on these lines:

(*i*) SIMPLE NARRATIVE.

   Much historical material
   Not all stageable: Henry's return to England (V)
   Bridging time-intervals (V)
   Gaps in story: French offer of dukedoms (III)
   Changes of place: to Southampton (II)

(*ii*) AROUSING EXPECTATION.

   Preparations for war (II)
   Future events: the conspiracy (II); the battle (IV)

(*iii*) INTERPRETATION.

   Making us see people and events in a certain light
   Henry: warlike Harry (Prol.), grace of kings (II)
   The English: culled and choice-drawn cavaliers (II)
   The conspirators: hollow bosoms (II)
   The French: afraid, pale policy (II); dicing for English (IV)

(*iv*) IMAGINATIVE RECREATION.

> Apologies for theatre: this unworthy scaffold (I)
> Audience to use imagination: your imaginary forces (I)
> Imaginative creation of scenes and events:
>> Sailing of the fleet (III)
>> Return of Henry to England (V)
>> The armies before Agincourt (IV)

(*v*) EPIC QUALITY.

> Narrative as in epic poems
> High style: many rhetorical figures
> Comparison of Henry to Roman emperor

It would be possible to add a concluding section, summarizing the five functions discussed; but this is not really necessary, since the structure of the essay is quite clear. It would also be possible to add an introductory section, explaining what the Chorus is; but it seems more reasonable to assume that the reader already knows this; and it is very effective and businesslike to begin the essay straight away with the first of the functions to be discussed.

Given this plan, the essay can be different lengths, according to the amount of detail and illustrative material. The following version includes a few more examples than the plan, and is almost exactly a thousand words long. Notice how much use can be made of very short quotations from the play; this is especially useful in examinations.

Specimen essay

'What are the functions of the Chorus in Henry V*?'*

The simplest function of the Chorus in *Henry V* is a straightforward story-telling one: the Chorus narrates parts of the story which Shakespeare does not wish to stage, bridges intervals of time, fills in gaps in the story, informs the audience of changes of place. Shakespeare's sources contained large amounts of historical material, much more than he could use in a play, and much of it not suitable for the stage. Some of this material is narrated by the Chorus, for example the French offer of some 'petty and unprofitable dukedoms' which Henry rejected (II.Chor.), and Henry's return to England after Agincourt (V.Chor.), and the visit of the Emperor to England on behalf of France (V.Chor.). The Chorus to Act V also illustrates the bridging of time-gaps: it explains that everything is going to be left out between Agincourt and Henry's return to France, and asks the audience to 'brook abridgment'. The use of the Chorus to indicate changes of place is seen in the Chorus to Act II, in which we are told that the scene is going to move to Southampton and then to France.

In addition to simple narration, the Chorus has the function of arousing the audience's expectation, whetting their appetite for what is to come. This is seen in the Prologue, which suggests the excitement of the great deeds which are to be seen in the play, and at the beginning of the Chorus to Act II, which describes the preparations for war, when 'honour's thought Reigns solely in the breast of every man'. This raising of expectation is achieved by looking forward to future events like the conspiracy against the king (II.Chor.) and the battle of Agincourt (IV.Chor.).

Thirdly, the Chorus influences the audience's attitudes to people and events; and this is a more important function. It does not simply narrate things, but interprets them, makes us see them in a certain light. Henry is consistently praised and presented favourably: he is 'the warlike Harry' (Prologue), 'this grace of kings' (II.Chor.), 'the Royal Captain of this ruined band' (IV.Chor.), 'This star of England' (Epilogue). There is a vivid description of his behaviour before Agincourt (IV.Chor.), going cheerfully and modestly around his troops, and of the piety of his behaviour after the battle (V.Chor.), when, free from 'vainness and self-glorious pride', he attributes the victory to God. The English army, similarly, are presented as 'culled and choice-drawn cavaliers' and 'English Mercuries' (II.Chor). The conspirators, on the other hand, are 'three corrupted men', 'a nest of hollow bosoms', and are impelled by 'hell and treason' (II.Chor.). When the French hear of Henry's military preparations, they 'shake in their fear', and try to avoid the conflict by means of 'pale policy' ((II.Chor.); before Agincourt, on the other hand, they are 'confident and over-lusty', and show their arrogance by dicing for the English prisoners they have not yet captured. In these ways, the Chorus insists on a certain interpretation of the historical events: it glorifies Henry and the English army, denigrates their enemies, and invites patriotic applause from the audience.

Fourthly, the Chorus encourages the audience to use their imagination, and itself creates various imaginative scenes and episodes in the story. There are frequent apologies for the inadequacy of the theatre to represent the great events of Henry's reign: it is 'this unworthy scaffold' (Prologue); its attempt to depict Agincourt will be a 'brawl ridiculous' carried out by 'four or five most vile and ragged foils' (IV.Chor.). The Chorus therefore constantly urges the audience to let the play operate on its 'imaginary forces', and to piece out the actor's imperfections with its thoughts (Prologue). The Chorus helps to achieve this by some magnificent set-pieces: it does not merely relate events, it re-creates them in the imagination of the audience. For example, there is the sailing of the English fleet from Southampton (III.Chor.), with the silken streamers fanning the sun, the ship-boys climbing in the 'hempen tackle', the 'shrill whistle' of the master or bo'sun of a ship, and the 'huge bottom' moving slowly through the water, like a city dancing on the 'inconstant billows'. Or again there is the vivid account of the crowds welcoming Henry when he landed at Dover, and when he arrived at Blackheath (V.Chor.). Above all, there is the superb account of the two armies the night before Agincourt (IV.Chor): the noises of the armies, the 'secret whispers' of the sentinels, the light from the camp-fires playing on men's faces, the cocks crowing and the clocks striking, the English sitting sadly by their fires with 'lank-lean cheeks and war-worn coats', looking in the moonlight like 'so many horrid ghosts'.

Finally, the Chorus contributes to the epic quality of the play. The very fact of containing long passages of narration makes the play more like an epic poem. Moreover, the style of the Chorus is high-pitched, often achieving epic grandeur. The tone is set immediately at the opening of the play, with the Prologue's combination of ardour with formal dignity:

O for a Muse of fire, that would ascend
The brightest heaven of invention,
A kingdom for a stage, princes to act,
And monarchs to behold the swelling scene.

The high style is achieved by an extensive use of figures, by elevated diction, by dignified comparisons. A good example of the epic quality conveyed by a comparison can be seen in the Chorus to Act V, when the Mayor and aldermen of London are compared to 'the senators of th'antique Rome', and Henry to their 'conquering Caesar'. This function of the Chorus, like the others, contributes to the overall purpose of the play—the celebration of the English monarchy and of the military qualities of the English.

Part 5

Suggestions for further reading

The text

The text of *Henry V* used in these *Notes* is the New Penguin:

SHAKESPEARE: *Henry V*, ed. A.R. Humphreys, Penguin Books, Harmondsworth, 1968.

There are two larger annotated editions which are specially recommended, namely the New Arden and the New Cambridge, which have full notes and long introductions:

SHAKESPEARE: *King Henry V*, ed. J.H. Walter, Methuen, London, 1954.

SHAKESPEARE: *King Henry V*, ed. J.D. Wilson, Cambridge University Press, London, 1947.

Other works by Shakespeare

There are innumerable editions of Shakespeare's collected works. The following is a convenient one-volume edition with a reliable text:

SHAKESPEARE: *The Complete Works*, ed. P. Alexander, Collins, London and Glasgow, 1951.

General works on Shakespeare

It is difficult to make recommendations from the thousands available. The following, however, are certainly useful:

HALLIDAY, F.E.: *A Shakespeare Companion*, Penguin Books, Harmondsworth, 1964.

HARRISON, G.B. *Introducing Shakespeare*, third edition, Penguin Books, Harmondsworth, 1966.

MUIR, K. and S. SCHOENBAUM: *A New Companion to Shakespeare Studies*, Cambridge University Press, London, 1971.

REESE, M.M. *Shakespeare: His World and His Work*, Edward Arnold, London, 1953.

Harrison is a very elementary introduction, while Reese is a much larger and more advanced book. Halliday is a reference-work, arranged under alphabetical headings. Muir and Schoenbaum contains eighteen articles on various topics, suitable for the more advanced student.

Dictionaries

The standard authority on the meanings of English words in the past is the big twelve-volume Oxford English Dictionary. More convenient for the elementary student of Shakespeare is

ONIONS, C.T.: *A Shakespeare Glossary*, second edition, Clarendon Press, Oxford, 1946.

Critical works

There is a very useful collection of critical articles on *Henry V*:

QUINN, M. (ed.): *Shakespeare, Henry V: a Casebook*, Macmillan, London, 1969.

This contains, among other things, the articles by Gould and Walters referred to in Part 2 above. More advanced students will find sections on *Henry V* in many other works, especially in books on the history plays; the following are recommended:

CAMPBELL, L.B.: *Shakespeare's 'Histories': Mirrors of Elizabethan Policy*, Huntingdon Library, San Marino, California, 1947.
KNIGHTS, L.C.: *Shakespeare: the Histories*, Longman, London, 1962.
MUIR, K.: ed., *Shakespeare Survey 30*, Cambridge University Press, Cambridge, 1977.
ORNSTEIN, R.: *A Kingdom for a Stage*, Harvard University Press, Cambridge, Mass., 1972.
PALMER, J.: *Political Characters of Shakespeare*, Macmillan, London, 1945.
PRIOR, M.E.: *The Drama of Power*, North-Western University Press, Evanston, Illinois, 1973.
REESE, M.M.: *The Cease of Majesty*, Edward Arnold, London, 1961.
RIBNER, I.: *The English History Play in the Age of Shakespeare*, Princeton University Press, Princeton, 1957.
TILLYARD, E.M.W.: *Shakespeare's History Plays*, Chatto and Windus, London, 1944.
TRAVERSI, D.A.: *Shakespeare: from Richard II to Henry V*, Hollis and Carter, London, 1958.
WILSON, J.D.: *The Fortunes of Falstaff*, Cambridge University Press, Cambridge, 1943.

On Shakespeare's imagery, consult the following:

CLEMEN, W.: *The Development of Shakespeare's Imagery*, second edition, Methuen, London, 1977.
SPURGEON, C.: *Shakespeare's Imagery*, Cambridge University Press, Cambridge, 1953.

Neither, however, says very much about *Henry V.*

Sources

For the sources of the play, consult the relevant portions of the following:

BULLOUGH, G.: *Narrative and Dramatic Sources of Shakespeare*, Vol. IV, Routledge and Kegan Paul, London, 1962.
MUIR, K.: *The Sources of Shakespeare's Plays*, Methuen, London, 1977.

Background works

An elementary account of the world-view of Shakespeare's time will be found in

TILLYARD, E.M.W.: *The Elizabethan World Picture*, Chatto and Windus, London, 1943.

For an account of the English language in Shakespeare's time, and the ways in which it differed from present-day English, see

BARBER, C.: *Early Modern English*, Deutsch, London, 1976.

On the theatres, companies, actors, and stage-conditions of Shakespeare's time, a useful though tightly-packed account is given by

GURR, A.: *The Shakespearean Stage 1574–1642*, Cambridge University Press, London, 1970.

The author of these notes

CHARLES BARBER was educated at St Catharine's College, Cambridge where he won the Charles Oldham Shakespeare Prize. After a year's teacher-training at the University of London, where he won the Storey-Miller Prize for Educational Theory, he became a teacher at a London grammar school. During the war he served in the Royal Air Force. He was then successively a lecturer in English at the University of Gothenburg, Sweden, and assistant lecturer in English at the Queen's University of Belfast. From 1959 until his retirement in 1980, he was at the University of Leeds, where he became a Reader in English Language and Literature, and Chairman of the School of English. His publications include an edition of Shakespeare's *Hamlet*, editions of three plays by Thomas Middleton, and a number of books on the English language, including a popular Pan paperback called *The Story of Language*. He is also the author of York Notes on Shakespeare's *As You Like It* and *Richard III*.

York Notes: list of titles

CHINUA ACHEBE
Things Fall Apart

EDWARD ALBEE
Who's Afraid of Virginia Woolf?

MARGARET ATWOOD
The Handmaid's Tale

W. H. AUDEN
Selected Poems

JANE AUSTEN
Emma
Mansfield Park
Northanger Abbey
Persuasion
Pride and Prejudice
Sense and Sensibility

SAMUEL BECKETT
Waiting for Godot

ARNOLD BENNETT
The Card

JOHN BETJEMAN
Selected Poems

WILLIAM BLAKE
Songs of Innocence, Songs of Experience

ROBERT BOLT
A Man For All Seasons

CHARLOTTE BRONTË
Jane Eyre

EMILY BRONTË
Wuthering Heights

BYRON
Selected Poems

GEOFFREY CHAUCER
The Clerk's Tale
The Franklin's Tale
The Knight's Tale
The Merchant's Tale
The Miller's Tale
The Nun's Priest's Tale
The Pardoner's Tale
Prologue to the Canterbury Tales
The Wife of Bath's Tale

SAMUEL TAYLOR COLERIDGE
Selected Poems

JOSEPH CONRAD
Heart of Darkness

DANIEL DEFOE
Moll Flanders
Robinson Crusoe

SHELAGH DELANEY
A Taste of Honey

CHARLES DICKENS
Bleak House
David Copperfield
Great Expectations
Hard Times
Oliver Twist

EMILY DICKINSON
Selected Poems

JOHN DONNE
Selected Poems

DOUGLAS DUNN
Selected Poems

GERALD DURRELL
My Family and Other Animals

GEORGE ELIOT
Middlemarch
The Mill on the Floss
Silas Marner

T. S. ELIOT
Four Quartets
Murder in the Cathedral
Selected Poems
The Waste Land

WILLIAM FAULKNER
The Sound and the Fury

HENRY FIELDING
Joseph Andrews
Tom Jones

F. SCOTT FITZGERALD
The Great Gatsby
Tender is the Night

GUSTAVE FLAUBERT
Madame Bovary

E. M. FORSTER
Howards End
A Passage to India

JOHN FOWLES
The French Lieutenant's Woman

ELIZABETH GASKELL
North and South

WILLIAM GOLDING
Lord of the Flies

GRAHAM GREENE
Brighton Rock
The Heart of the Matter
The Power and the Glory

THOMAS HARDY
Far from the Madding Crowd
Jude the Obscure
The Mayor of Casterbridge
The Return of the Native
Selected Poems
Tess of the D'Urbervilles

L. P. HARTLEY
The Go-Between

NATHANIEL HAWTHORNE
The Scarlet Letter

SEAMUS HEANEY
Selected Poems

ERNEST HEMINGWAY
A Farewell to Arms
The Old Man and the Sea

SUSAN HILL
I'm the King of the Castle

HOMER
The Iliad
The Odyssey

GERARD MANLEY HOPKINS
Selected Poems

TED HUGHES
Selected Poems

ALDOUS HUXLEY
Brave New World

HENRY JAMES
The Portrait of a Lady

BEN JONSON
The Alchemist
Volpone

JAMES JOYCE
Dubliners
A Portrait of the Artist as a Young Man

JOHN KEATS
Selected Poems

PHILIP LARKIN
Selected Poems

D. H. LAWRENCE
The Rainbow
Selected Short Stories
Sons and Lovers
Women in Love

HARPER LEE
To Kill a Mockingbird

LAURIE LEE
Cider with Rosie

CHRISTOPHER MARLOWE
Doctor Faustus

ARTHUR MILLER
The Crucible
Death of a Salesman
A View from the Bridge

JOHN MILTON
Paradise Lost I & II
Paradise Lost IV & IX

SEAN O'CASEY
Juno and the Paycock

GEORGE ORWELL
Animal Farm
Nineteen Eighty-four

JOHN OSBORNE
Look Back in Anger

WILFRED OWEN
Selected Poems

HAROLD PINTER
The Caretaker

SYLVIA PLATH
Selected Works

ALEXANDER POPE
Selected Poems

J. B. PRIESTLEY
An Inspector Calls

WILLIAM SHAKESPEARE
Antony and Cleopatra
As You Like It
Coriolanus
Hamlet
Henry IV Part I
Henry IV Part II
Henry V
Julius Caesar
King Lear
Macbeth
Measure for Measure
The Merchant of Venice
A Midsummer Night's Dream
Much Ado About Nothing
Othello
Richard II
Richard III
Romeo and Juliet
Sonnets
The Taming of the Shrew
The Tempest

Troilus and Cressida
Twelfth Night
The Winter's Tale

GEORGE BERNARD SHAW
Arms and the Man
Pygmalion
Saint Joan

MARY SHELLEY
Frankenstein

PERCY BYSSHE SHELLEY
Selected Poems

RICHARD BRINSLEY SHERIDAN
The Rivals

R. C. SHERRIFF
Journey's End

JOHN STEINBECK
The Grapes of Wrath
Of Mice and Men
The Pearl

TOM STOPPARD
Rosencrantz and Guildenstern are Dead

JONATHAN SWIFT
Gulliver's Travels

JOHN MILLINGTON SYNGE
The Playboy of the Western World

W. M. THACKERAY
Vanity Fair

MARK TWAIN
Huckleberry Finn

VIRGIL
The Aeneid

DEREK WALCOTT
Selected Poems

ALICE WALKER
The Color Purple

JOHN WEBSTER
The Duchess of Malfi

OSCAR WILDE
The Importance of Being Earnest

THORNTON WILDER
Our Town

TENNESSEE WILLIAMS
The Glass Menagerie

VIRGINIA WOOLF
Mrs Dalloway
To the Lighthouse

WILLIAM WORDSWORTH
Selected Poems

W. B. YEATS
Selected Poems